160 Questions on the Kabbalah

Answers to your questions and more ...

Rabbi Raphael Afilalo

From the same author

The Kabbalah of the Ari Z'al, according to the Ramhal
Kabbalah Editions

Kabbalah Dictionary
Kabbalah Editions

Kabbalah Glossary
Kabbalah Editions

Kabbalists and their works
Kabbalah Editions

160 Questions on the Kabbalah
Kabbalah Editions

Kabbalah concepts
Kabbalah Editions

Kabbalah Editions, 2005 – www.kabbalaheditions.com
www.ravraphael.com
www.kabbalah5.com
rav@kabbalah5.com
ravraphael@yahoo.com

Publisher's Cataloging-in-Publication
Afilalo, Raphael
    160 Questions on the Kabbalah: An introduction to the
    terms and concepts of the Kabbalah / Raphael Afilalo
p.cm.
Includes bibliographical references and index.
ISBN 2923241096 (Soft cover)
1.Cabala. 2. Mysticism—Judaism. I. Afilalo, Raphael. II. Title.
BM525. BM723 2005
296.1'6   2005937754

מרדכי אליהו

MORDECHAI ELIAHU
FORMER CHIEF RABBI OF ISRAEL & RICHON LEZION

הראשון לציון ורבה הראשי לישראל לשעבר

APPROBATION

דוד רפאל באנון
DAVID R. BANON
RABBIN DU CENTRE SÉPHARADE DE LAVAL
MEMBRE DU BETH DIN DE MONTRÉAL
חבר בית הדין

RABBI DAVID HANANIA PINTO
Rehov Bayit Vegan 97
Jerusalem - Israël
Tel: (972-2) 643 3605
Fax: (972-2) 641 3945 - 643 3570

דוד חנניה פינטו
רחוב בית וגן 97
ירושלים - ישראל
טל: 6433605
6413945 6433570
4773, Rue Clanranald - Chomedey Laval - P.Q. (CANADA) Tel. (450) 681-6412, Fax (514) 342-

בע"ה יום חמישי לסדר "וישב" תשס"ז

שלום וברכה

המלצה

באתי בזאת להמליץ על הספר "Kabalah Dictionary"
(מילון הקבלה) שכתב הרב רפאל אפללו שליט"א. בספר הנ"ל
יש הגדרות ומונחים על קבלת הרמח"ל זיע"א הכל מסודר
בצורה טה נוחה ללימוד ולעיון בו.

לאור התהמלצות חרבות שקיבל הספר, נשאר לי רק להמליץ
עליו בכל לב.

אני מברך בזכות אבותי וקדושים זיע"א את המחובר שליט"א
לברכה והצלחה ושיזכה להוציא מתחת ידיו עוד ספרים לזכות
הרבים ושיתעלה מעלה בתוה"ק ויראת שמים. אמן

ע"ה דוד חנניה פינטו ס"ט

דוד חנניה פינטו
רחוב בית וגן 97
ירושלים - ישראל
טל: 643 3605
02 641 3945 - 02 643 3605 פקס:

מוסדות אורות חיים ומשה
רחוב האדמו"ר מבעלז 617
אשדוד - ישראל
08 853 1827 טל:
08 852 6152 פקס:

OHR HAIM VÉMOCHÉ
11, Rue Du Plateau
75019 Paris • France
Tel: (33-1) 42 08 25 40
Fax: (33-1) 42 08 50 85

YECHIVA PINTO
26 Bis, Rue Des Mûriers
69100 Villeurbanne
France
Tel: (33-4) 78 03 89 14

הרבנות הראשית רמלה
08-9225368
VILLE ANONYME
רחוב הרצל 48 ת.ד. 4 רמלה טל. בית 8221233-08

To my son David

Table of contents

Introduction 15

KABBALAH – GENERAL 28 Questions 17

1   *What does the word Kabbalah mean?* 19
2   *What is Kabbalah?* 19
3   *What does it mean "to receive"?* 19
4   *What are the subjects covered in the Kabbalah?* 20
5   *What are the writings that make the Kabbalah?*. 20
6   *What is "Practical Kabbalah"?* 20
7   *What is the history of the Kabbalah?* 21
8   *What is a Kabbalist?* 22
9   *Who are some of the most important Kabbalists?*
     23
10   *How about Madonna, Kabbalah and show*
business? 25
11   *What is the "Tree of life"?* 26
12   *What is the "Tree of death"?* 27
13   *What is "ATBaSH"?* 27
14   *What is "Notrikun"?* 27
15   *What is a Kmi'a (Amulet)?* 27
16   *Why is there free will for men?* 28
17   *What are the good and bad impulse in man?* 29
18   *What is the Garden of Eden?* 29
19   *What is the lower Gan 'Eden?* 30
20   *What is the higher Gan 'Eden?* 30
21   *What is time in the Kabbalah?* 30
22   *What difference is there for each day?* 30
23   *What is a Yi'hud (unification)?* 31
24   *Is there creation from nothing?* 31

25   *How is each Jew a guarantor for his fellow Jew?*32

26   *How is man at the image of the supernal form?* . 32

27   *What is the name of 72?* 32

28   *What are the different levels of prophecy?* 33

LEARNING KABBALAH 22 Questions 35

29   *What do we learn in the Kabbalah?* 37

30   *How can one start to learn the Kabbalah?* 38

31   *Why should I learn the Kabbalah?* 38

32   *What have the rabbinical authorities declared about learning the Kabbalah?* 39

33   *What does the Zohar say about learning the Kabbalah?* 40

34   *Why has the study of Kabbalah been discouraged by some?* 40

35   *Is it not forbidden to study the Kabbalah before the age of forty?* 41

36   *Can women study Kabbalah?* 42

37   *Can non-Jews study the Kabbalah?* 42

38   *Does the learning of the Kabbalah require a certain way of life?* 43

39   *Why are names of body parts used to describe higher lights?* 43

40   *What is the essential knowledge?* 43

41   *What is the Torah in the Kabbalah?* 44

42   *What is "Ma'ase Bereshit"?* 45

43   *What is "Ma'ase HaMerkava"?* 45

44   *What is the Merkava (heavenly chariot)?* 45

45   *What is the role of the Hebrew letters (Autiot)?* .. 45

46   *How is G-od unique and yet have so many attributes?* 46

47   *Why is G-od called "Ein Sof" (Infinite) in the Kabbalah?* 47

48   *When is the name of G-od; "Elohi-m" used?* 47

49   *What is the Zohar?* 47

50   *Who is the Ari Z'al?* 48

8

CREATION 10 Questions 49

51   *What is the Hishtalshelut – (chain of events)?* ... 51
52   *What is the Tsimtsum - (retraction)?* 51
53   *What is the 'Hallal – (vacant space)?* 51
54   *What is the Reshimu - (imprint)?* 52
55   *What is the Kav – (ray)?* 52
56   *Why are the letters of the name of G-od spelled
differently?* 52
57   *What are the Sephirot of the name of BaN (52)?* 53
58   *What is the Shvirat HaKelim - breaking of the
vessels?* 54
59   *What are the Rapa'h Nitsutsot - (288 Sparks)?* .. 55
60   *What are the Sephirot of MaH (45)* 56

WORLDS 8 Questions 57

61   *What is a world?* 59
62   *How many worlds are there?* 59
63   *What is the difference between these worlds?* ... 59
64   *What is Atsilut?* 59
65   *What is Beriah?* 60
66   *What is Yetsirah?* 60
67   What is 'Asiah? 60
68   *What are the types of existence in our world?* ... 61

SEPHIROT 20 Questions 63

69   *What is a Sephira ?* 65
70   *How many Sephirot are there and what are their
names?* 65
71   *What is a Sephirotic tree?* 66
72   *What are the Sephirot Ha'Igulim - (encircling
Sephirot)?* 68
73   *What are the Sephirot HaYashar - (linear
Sephirot)?* 68
74   *What is Adam Kadmon - (Primordial man)?* 68
75   *What are the NeHY?* 69
76   *What are the 'HaGaT?* 69
77   *What are the 'HaBaD?* 69
78   *What is the Sephira Keter - (crown)?* 70

79 *What is the Sephira 'Hokhma - (wisdom)?* 70

80 *What is the Sephira Binah - (understanding)?*....71

81 *What is the Sephira Da'at - (Knowledge)?*..........71

82 *What is the Sephira 'Hesed - (bounty)?* 72

83 *What is the Sephira Gevurah - (rigor)?*...............72

84 *What is the Sephira Tiferet - (beauty)?*...............73

85 *What is the Sephira Netsa'h - (splendor)?*..........73

86 *What is the Sephira Hod - (glory)?* 74

87 *What is the Sephira Yesod - (foundation)?*.........74

88 *What is the Sephira Malkhut - (royalty)?*............75

PARTSUFIM 18 Questions 77

89 *What is a PARTSUF – (configuration)?* 79

90 *What are the different types of configurations?* ..79

91 *What are the actions of a Partsuf?* 79

92 *Do their actions or interactions vary?* 80

93 *What are the names of the Partsufim?* 80

94 *From which Sephirot do the Partsufim emerge?* 81

95 *What is Partsuf 'Atik Yomin?* 82

96 *What is the role of Partsuf 'Atik Yomin?* 82

97 *What is Partsuf Arikh Anpin?*.............................82

98 *What are the Partsufim (configurations) Abah and Imah?* 83

99 *What is Partsuf Zeir Anpin?*...............................83

100 *What is the role of Partsuf Zeir Anpin?*...........83

101 *What is Partsuf Nukvah ?* 84

102 *What is the role of Partsuf Nukvah?* 85

103 *What are the Mo'hin of a configuration?*........85

104 *What is a Zivug - (union)?*...............................86

105 *What are the different types of Zivugim?*........86

106 *What are the different positions of the configurations?*..87

GUIDANCE 8 Questions...89

107 *What are the types of guidance?*....................91

108 *By which attributes or qualities is the guidance manifested?*...91

109 *What is the attribute of Kindness?*..................91

110 *What is the attribute of Judgment?*.................92

111   *What is the attribute of mercy?*...................... 92
112   *How is the Guidance manifested?*................. 93
113   *What is the will to bestow?* 93
114   *What is the "desire to receive"?*..................... 94

MITSVOT 3 Questions... 95

115   *What are the Mitsvot (commandments) in the Kabbalah?*.. 97
116   *What is the relation between the Mitsvot and the Sephirot?* 97
117   *What is the goal of the Mitsvot?* 98

PRAYER 9 Questions.. 99

118   *What is a Tefilah (prayer)?* 101
119   *Why do we have to pray everyday?* 101
120   *What is the role of the prayers?* 102
121   *What is the goal of the different blessings?*.. 102
122   *Why do we do a blessing before, and after eating something?* 103
123   *What is a Hekhal - (portal)?*.......................... 103
124   *What are the names and the correspondence of the Hekhalot (portals)?* 103
125   *What is "Kavanah" - (concentration)?*.......... 104
126   *What is the goal of the Kavanot?* 104

TIKUN 9 Questions... 107

127   *What is a Tikun – (rectification – action)?* 109
128   *What was the first Tikun to repair the worlds?* 109
129   *How were the broken Sephirot repaired?*..... 109
130   *How are the Tikunim of the configurations realized?* 110
131   What are the *Tikunim* of the *Partsufim* for the guidance? 110
132   *What is a Tikun for a soul?*........................... 110
133   What is *Tikun 'Olam* – general *Tikun?* 111

11

134   How do we participate in the ascent of the 288 sparks?... 111
135   *What is the final goal of the reunification of the sparks?*... 112

SOULS 5 Questions... 113

136   *What is the soul in the Kabbalah?* 115
137   *Are there different "qualities" of souls?* 115
138   *What are the different roots of the souls?*..... 115
139   *How are the higher levels of the souls acquired?* 116
140   *What are the different levels of the soul?* 117

REINCARNATION 7 Questions 119

141   *Does reincarnation exist?* 121
142   *What is a Gilgul (reincarnation)?* 121
143   *What is a 'Ibur (attachment of a soul)?* 121
144   *How many time can a soul reincarnate?*....... 122
145   *Why does a soul need to reincarnate?* 122
146   *Can a soul reincarnate in an other form?* 122
147   *Will there be resurrection of the dead?*......... 123

NEGATIVE FORCE 5 Questions 125

148   *What is the "Sitra A'hra" (Negative force)?*.. 127
149   *Why is there a "Negative force"?* 127
150   *How does the "Negative force" get strength?*128
151   *What are the Klipot - (husks)?* 128
152   *What are the different levels of Klipot?*......... 128

ANGELS 6 Questions 129

153   *What is an angel?* 131
154   *What are the different types of angels?*........ 131
155   *How many groups of angels are there?*........ 131
156   *Are there negative angels?*........................... 132
157   *Do angels have free choice?* 132
158   *Are men superior to angels?*......................... 132

GEMATRIA 2 Questions 133

159   *What is Gematria?* 135
160   *How many types of Gematriot are there?* 135

Transliteration of the letters 139
GLOSSARY 141
Index 181
TABLES 185

Introduction

During the lectures or conferences, I have given in various places and for different types of listeners; I realized that people always have a lot of questions on the Kabbalah. Sometimes, the time allowed for the questions was stretched even more than the length of the lecture itself. It happened often, that we had to put an end to the questions period that was extending too late.

I have noticed that some general questions about the Kabbalah were asked over and over, as well as specific questions about man, the Creator, the Jewish rituals, life and death, the esoteric and hidden knowledge and more. Also, more specific questions by more experienced learners, about the creation and the guidance have also been asked.

In this book, I have tried to answer most of these questions in a short, simple and concise language. I have also added at the end, a general glossary for other terms and concepts. For deeper explanations of the essential terms and concepts most often encountered in the Kabbalah, I will suggest the "Kabbalah Dictionary[1]" or the "Kabbalah Concepts[2]" as a second step.

I would like to thank my wife Simona for her patience and encouragements, and my brother Armand, for his friendship and constant support.

---

[1] Kabbalah Dictionary, Rabbi Raphael Afilalo, Kabbalah Editions
[2] Kabbalah Concepts, Rabbi Raphael Afilalo, Kabbalah Editions

KABBALAH – GENERAL

28 Questions

1   ***What does the word Kabbalah mean?***

The word Kabbalah has its root in the Hebrew verb *Lekabel* - to receive. It can also mean to accept or be accepted.

2   ***What is Kabbalah?***

The Kabbalah is the Jewish mystical and esoteric wisdom. It teaches the unfolding of the worlds, the various ways of guidance of these worlds, the role of man in the creation, the will of the Creator and so on. No other writings explain in details; the creation of this world and the ones above it, the lights or energies that influence its guidance, nor the final goal of everything. These writings are based on the Torah, on ancient and newer Jewish texts, and mostly on the Zohar.

3   ***What does it mean "to receive"?***

Kabbalah comes from the verb *Lekabel* (to receive), but to receive, it is first necessary to want, and to become a *Keli* (recipient) able to receive and contain this knowledge. A person has to merit and be accepted to receive this knowledge, and hold it by living in the path of *Torah* and rightness to strengthen himself constantly.

4   *What are the subjects covered in the Kabbalah?*

Beside the main subjects covered in the Kabbalah as the unfolding of the worlds and their guidance, the real meaning and goals of the *Mitsvot*[3] and prayers, it comprises of numerous other sciences as: astrology, cosmology, *Gematria*[4], metaphysics, demonology, physiognomy, palmistry, healing, alchemy, reincarnation, exorcism, prophecy etc.

5   *What are the writings that make the Kabbalah?*

The base of all the writings of the Kabbalah is the Zohar, written in the second century by Rabbi Shim'on Bar Yo'hai. Other important works are the "Sepher HaYetsira" - the Book of Formation, Kitve HaAri" – the Writings of the Ari Z'al etc. All these writings try to explain and comment on the secrets hidden and alluded in the Torah.

6   *What is "Practical Kabbalah"?*

It is the "other" type of Kabbalah, where names or combinations of names of angels are used with special signs or incantations, sometimes written on parchment, to invoke particular powers and alter normal states of events

---

[3] Commandments
[4] Numerology

7   *What is the history of the Kabbalah?*

The first book that mentions a system of ten lights called *Sephirot* is "*Sepher HaYetsira*" - The Book of Formation, is attributed to Avraham Avinu (Aprox. 1750 B.C.E)

During the second century, Rabbi Shim'on Bar Yo'hai composed the Zohar which is the esoteric and mystical explanation of the Torah, and the base of most of the Kabbalah writings.

In the twelfth century, after having disappeared for about one thousand years, the book of the Zohar is found and printed by Rabbi Moshe de Leon in Spain.

In Europe during the twelfth and thirteenth centuries, in the cities of Provence in France, Gerona in Spain and Worms in Germany were formed three of the main centers of Kabbalah of that period. It is also the period of the "Prophetic Kabbalah" as taught by Rabbi Abraham Abul'afia.

After the expulsion from Spain in 1492, was founded in the city of Tsfat in Israel, a school of Kabbalah named "New Kabbalah" or "Kabbalah of Tsfat", it is the golden period of the Kabbalah under Rabbi Its'hak Luria Ashkenazi; the Ari Z'al.

During the 16th century with the coming of Shabbetai Tsevi who was called the "Kabbalistic Messiah", the Jewish community was divided between his followers and the non-believers. After converting to Islam, this false Messiah caused a big deception and mistrust in the teachings of the Kabbalah. The rabbinical authorities of the time became even more severe with the learning of Kabbalah and some were persecuted for learning or writing on the subject.

During the seventeenth and eighteenth centuries, the Kabbalah becomes more popular in east Europe with the *'Hassidic* movements. Their founder; the Ba'al Shem Tov and others, try to give the possibility to every Jew to get closer to his creator, by becoming more spiritual and studying with more profundity.

In the beginning of this century, Rabbi Yehudah Ashlag translated all the Zohar from Aramaic to Hebrew, this allowed an even better dissemination of its teachings.

8   *What is a Kabbalist?*

As said above, the word Kabbalah comes from the verb *Lekabel* (to receive), but to receive it is first necessary to be prepared, and to be a *Keli* (recipient) able to receive and contain this knowledge.

A Kabbalist is a person who is accepted to receive this knowledge, and is able to hold it by living in the path of Torah and rightness to strengthen himself constantly. He is a spiritual person who will give utmost importance to the higher meaning of things, and continually try to advance in his learning. For him, the main goal of this existence is to get closer to the Creator and serve him to the best of his possibilities.

9   *Who are some of the most important Kabbalists?*

Rabbi Shim'on Bar Yo'hai lived in Galilee in the second century, he composed the Zohar which is the esoteric and mystical explanation of the Torah, and the base of most of the Kabbalah writings.

Rabbi Moshe de Leon who reprinted the Zohar after it had disappeared for a thousand years. (1270)

The heads of the three Kabbalah schools in Europe: Rabbi Its'hak the Blind in France, Rabbi Ezra of Gerona in Spain and Rabbi El'azar of Worms, in Germany. (1200)

Rabbi Abraham Abul'afia and Rabbi Yosef Giktalia. They created the school of "Prophetic Kabbalah". (1200 – 1300)

The first generation of the Kabbalists of Tsfat in Israel: Rabbi Moshe Kordovero, Rabbi Shlomo Alkabetz and Rabbi Yoseph Karo. After this first generation, Rabbi Its'hak Luria Ashkenazi; the Ari Z'al became the leading Kabbalist in Tsfat. He explained and clarified all the main concepts of the Kabbalah, and also innovated in the explanation of the Sephirot and Partsufim (configurations). He is the author of the corpus "'*Ets 'Haim*" which is today the major reference in Kabbalah. (1500)

The Ba'al Shem Tov was the founder of the *'Hassidic* movement, his teachings were largely based upon the Kabalistic teachings of the Ari Z'al, but his approach made the benefits of these teachings accessible even to the simplest Jew. Some of the other important leaders that founded their own *'Hassidic* movement are Rabbi Na'hman of Breslev, great grandson of the Baal Shem Tov, Rabbi Shneur Zalman of Liadi, the *"Ba'al HaTanya"*, founder of the 'Habad Lubavitch movement. (1600 – 1700)

Rabbi Moshe 'Haim Luzzatto – Ram'hal who lived in Italy and Amsterdam. He was a very prolific writer and wrote on all the aspects of the Torah and the Kabbalah, but because of false accusations, was sadly persecuted for most of his short life. (1700)

Rabbi Eliyahu of Vilna - The Gaon of Vilna who was born in Lithuania. He was one of the main leaders of the *Mitnagdim* (opponents to the *'Hasidic* movement). He is considered to be one of the greatest Torah scholar and Kabbalist of the past two centuries. (1700)

Rabbi Shalom Shar'abi - The Rashash. He is known as the "Master of the *Kavanot*"[5]. His *"Siddur HaRashash"* is the *Siddur*[6] used by some Kabbalists in their everyday prayers, and is based on the *Kavanot* of the Ari Z'al. (1700)

Rabbi Ya'acov Abe'htsera was a Kabbalist renowned for his piety and for performing miracles. He composed works on all facets of the Torah including important commentaries on the Kabbalistic explanations of the Torah. (1800)

Rabbi 'Haim Ben 'Atar – Or Ha'Haim. The Ba'al Shem Tov was convinced that the Or Ha'Haim was the Moshia'h of that generation. His main work is the commentary on the Torah; "Or Ha'Haim" where he commented the Torah on the four

---

[5] Praying with concentration and with the permutation of names.
[6] Prayer book

levels of comprehension, from the *Pshat* (simple), to the Kabbalistic meaning. (1800)

Rabbi Yosef 'Haim –The Ben Ish 'Hai. He was a prolific author who wrote at incredible speed. It is known that he would finish writing a complete page before the ink at the top of the page had dried. He explained the *Halakhot* (laws) on the Kabbalistic level but in an accessible language. (1900)

Rabbi Yehudah Ashlag. His main work is the translation of all the Zohar from Aramaic to Hebrew called *"HaSulam"*[7]. (1950)

This list is not exhaustive, but each one of these great Kabbalah scholars brought his own explanations and innovations to the Kabbalah.

10   *How about Madonna, Kabbalah and show business?*

For some Kabbalah has become a "show business" word. If you learn Kabbalah, you belong to the same circle of friends as Madonna, Britney Spears, Demi Moore, Elizabeth Taylor etc. Today, these and other show business personalities claim to study Jewish mysticism; the Kabbalah.

In a recent interview on CNN, Madonna declared: "I am a Kabbalist, there is definitely a Kabbalistic approach to life, or a Kabbalistic point of view…"

---

[7] The ladder

Is it possible to study Kabbalah so easily and claim to be a Kabbalist? Or could the actual enchantment manifested by Madonna and others, be only momentary or a fade, knowing the intensity and the necessary investment required to study the authentic Kabbalah?

Wanting to get closer to G-od is very noble, and this, from whatever religion or background. I am sure that Madonna and the others sincerely want to do good, as she also declared: "I also believe that all paths lead to G-od". The problem is the people that allegedly show these seekers "the way" and take (a lot of) their money on the way. When we see Madonna flashing Hebrew names of G-od (which normally are so saintly that they should not even be pronounced) on the back wall of her rock concert, we wonder if she realizes the gravity of her actions.

If Madonna thinks that she is a Kabbalist, she is certainly not. If her teachers told her she was, they do not go by any recognized standards, and I personally think that she is being taken advantage of, because if she really wants to learn the authentic Kabbalah she would have to be taught very differently.

Her main contribution is the greater awareness of a very beautiful and powerful Jewish mysticism.

11   *What is the "Tree of life"?*

During the night the "Tree of Life" ascends higher and the "Tree of death" governs. According to the *Zohar,* it is only in the morning that the governance is given back to the Tree of Life and that all the souls return in men's bodies. (Zohar, Bamidbar)

It is also the name of the master work of the Ari Z'al.

12   *What is the "Tree of death"?*

During the night the "Tree of Life" ascends higher, the souls leave the bodies and the "Tree of death" governs.

13   *What is "ATBaSH"?*

It is a permutation of the letters of a word to understand its hidden meanings. The first letter is replaced by the last, second by the before last etc.

א by ת - ב by ש etc.

14   *What is "Notrikun"?*

Notrikun is a method of interpretation in which initials of different words make a new word.

אל מלך נאמן = אמן

15   *What is a Kmi'a (Amulet)?*

Names, or combinations of names of angels with special signs or incantations, written on parchment to protect, or to invoke particular powers.

By writing various permutation of letters or names of angels, one could make these superior forces act according to his will. There is danger of using these names without a proper preparation and a good knowledge of their forces and limits.

16   *Why is there free will for men?*

Since the intention of the Creator is to bestow goodness on His creatures, all the levels of creation were put in place so His kindness could emanate to them, yet in such a way that they would be able to receive it. Complete rigor will be the destruction of anything not perfect, while complete kindness will permit everything without restriction. However, these two aspects are necessary to make the guidance of kindness and justice and to give man the possibility of serving the Creator by their free will.

After the *Shvirat HaKelim* (breaking of the vessels) with the emanation of the lights of the name *MaH (45)* and *BaN (52)*, G-od could have done the *Tikun* (repair) of all the worlds, but then, there would not have been a reason for the participation of man in this *Tikun* and a possibility to acquire merit.

For man to have a possibility to act and repair the creation, G-od restrained in a way, his outflow of kindness to this world, to give men the merit of doing the *Tikun* with their free will. It is by their free will to get closer to their Creator and learn His ways, that men merit their place in the higher worlds when they depart.

17   *What are the good and bad impulse in man?*

The *Yetser Hatov* corresponds to the good or positive impulse in man, the *Yetser Hara'* is his bad or negative impulse.

The good deeds of man have an effect on the four higher worlds, his bad deeds; on the four lower worlds. It is only when man sins, that the negative side can grow in strength. The negative aspect grows inside him; this is his *Yetser Hara',* it cuts him off from the higher worlds, and uproots him from the *Kedushah*[8].

The *Yetser Hara'* almost constantly tries to seduce him, and make him stumble, while the *Yetser Hatov,* on the other side, tries to attract him to *Torah* and *Mitsvot*[9] and to help him do the *Tikun* (rectification) of his *Neshama*[10].

The two aspects of *Yetser Tov* and *Yetser Hara'* were created to allow man to choose good over bad by his own free choice.

18   *What is the Garden of Eden?*

It is the place of rest for the *Neshamot* (souls) after their separation with their former physical bodies. There is a lower and a higher *Gan 'Eden.*

---

[8] Holiness
[9] Commandments of the Torah
[10] Soul

19   *What is the lower Gan 'Eden?*

In the lower *Gan 'Eden*, the *Neshamot* (souls) are enjoying spiritual pleasures but still have a spiritual body resembling their former bodies.

.

20   *What is the higher Gan 'Eden?*

In the higher *Gan 'Eden*, the *Neshamot* (souls) are enjoying pure spiritual pleasures, and do not have any spiritual image resembling their former bodies

21   *What is time in the Kabbalah?*

There is a higher dimension where there is not a notion called time. Past, present and future are one. Man being a limited entity physically and temporally, it is not possible for him to comprehend this reality.

Everything, past, present and future has a purpose, and in the end, all that is and happens, will be clear and comprehensible.

22   What difference is there for each day?

Each new day, is of a new emanation that governs it. For each day, there are new *Zivugim* (unions) of different aspects of *Z"uN (Zeir Anpin and Nukvah)*[11].

---

[11] Masculine and feminine configurations of *Sephirot*

Each day, according to the actions of man, the *Tefilot*[12] during the week, *Shabbat* or Holidays, and depending on time, various configurations allow different *Zivugim* - unions, and therefore outflows of abundance of variable intensities.

Each day can also be described in term of permutation of the names of G-od, and by the various *Sephirot and Partsufim* – configurations that govern on this day.

23   *What is a Yi'hud (unification)?*

A *Yi'hud* is the unification of names or letters, as to provoke a specific action or reaction. In his book *"Sha'ar Rua'h HaKodesh"* the Ari Z'al explains the significance of the *Yi'hudim*, their different actions, and also warns of the danger of using these names without a proper preparation. By concentrating on various permutation of letters or names of angels, one could make these superior forces act according to his will.

The union of the *Sephirot* and configurations for the descent of the abundance is also called *Yi'hud*.

24   *Is there creation from nothing?*

There is a special force called *"Tsu'r T'K"*, which has the power to create separate entities from nothing.

---

[12] Prayers

This force is not related to the *Sephirot*. It was first explained in the "*Sepher HaYetsrira*"[13], which is the oldest Kabbalistic writing. It is only after being created that the guidance is taken over by the *Sephirot*.

25   *How is each Jew a guarantor for his fellow Jew?*

"*Kol Israel 'Arevim ze la ze*", every Jew is a guarantor for his fellow Jew. The majority of the *Tikunim* (rectifications), as explained in the Kabbalah, are not realized by one, but more by the actions of many. The *Geulah* (liberation) will come as a result of the efforts of all Israel.

26   *How is man at the image of the supernal form?*

Man is as the image of the *Sephirotic* tree and the higher lights, his soul has 613 parts and he has 248 limbs and 365 veins for a total of 613. Correspondingly, a *Sephira* or a configuration comprise of 613 main forces or lights, which afterward divide into many parts. This structure is also similar in the Torah, which has 248 positive and 365 negative commandments.

27   *What is the name of 72?*

The name of '*A"V* (72) is made of seventy two triplets of letters from three verses of the *Torah*.

---

[13] "Book of Formation" attributed to Abraham

It is hinted in the book of *Shemot*[14] chapt 14, from the three *Pesukim* (verses) 18, 19, 20, which have 72 letters each. From these three verses, we take the first letter of verse 18, the last letter of verse 19, the first letter of verse 20, than the second of verse 18, the before last of verse 19 and the second of verse 20, and so on to get 72 triplets. Each one of these triplets of letters, as explained in the *Zohar,* has particular powers.

28 *What are the different levels of prophecy?*

The prophecy originates from the *Sephira Netsa'h* or the *Sephira Hod*. These *Sephirot* have three parts each. The difference between the levels of the prophets, depends from which one of the three parts of these *Sephirot*, they receive the prophecy.

---

[14] Exodus

LEARNING KABBALAH

22 Questions

29   *What do we learn in the Kabbalah?*

In the Kabbalah we learn how and why G-od created the world, in what way He governs it, the provenance of the souls and angels, the purpose of the existence of evil, the systems that are put in place for the true guidance of the worlds, and more.

The Kabbalah teaches the unfolding of the worlds, the various powers of influence on these worlds, the role of man in the creation, the will of the Creator and so on. It explains in details; the creation of the present and previous worlds, the different lights or energies that make their guidance, the final goal of man and the creation.

The Kabbalah explains to us that the world is guided by an extremely complex system of forces or lights, which through their interactions provoke chain reactions that impact directly on man and the worlds. Each one of these reactions has numerous ramifications, with many details and results.

The Kabbalah also demonstrates to us the importance of man, because only he, by getting closer to the Creator, can influence these incredible forces. For this, one has to elevate to a higher dimension of understanding, and start asking himself some very important questions like; "Why", "What is the purpose of doing this act or this prayer", "What are the outcomes of my actions" etc.

In the Kabbalah, one can find all these answers and the exact reasons, and effects of all our rituals, prayers and actions. When one decides that he wants to know his Creator, in learning this science he ascends to a higher level of action and superior understanding and thus live and feel a more intense relation with his Creator. He will also realize his smallness compared to these incredible forces, the perfection of the Lord and His infinite love for His creatures.

30   *How can one start to learn the Kabbalah?*

The first step is starting to learn the Torah, the *Halakhot*[15], the different prayers, adopt an adequate behavior and preferably develop a good knowledge of Hebrew. The second step is to find an experienced and knowledgeable rabbi to learn with.

31   *Why should I learn the Kabbalah?*

Firstly, to understand what is expected of me, how I can better accomplish His commandments, the purpose of my prayers and actions. Secondly, to get closer to my creator by learning His ways, and understanding the different emanations of His lights and powers in this world, and the others. Thirdly, to "connect" with G-od, by deepening my understanding of His presence and manifestation in this existence, to have a fuller spiritual life and find meaning to our lives. Through the knowledge of Kabbalah, one can get to a level of true understanding, and in a way "decode" the profound secrets of this existence as found in our holy Torah.

---

[15] Jewish laws and customs

32   *What have the rabbinical authorities declared about learning the Kabbalah?*

Rabbi Shneur Zalman of Liadi, (Ba'al HaTania), the founder of the Lubavitch movement said:

"The knowledge of the Kabbalah was hidden in those times and concealed for all these *"Talmide 'Hakhamim"*[16], except for a few, and even then, discreetly in small groups and not in public as the Gemarah. But as the Ari Z'al wrote; especially now for these last generations, it is allowed and a *"Mitsvah"*[17] to reveal this science."
(Agarot HaKodesh, 26).

The Gaon de Vilna said:
"The one, who was able to learn the secrets of the Torah (Kabbalah) and did not make an effort to understand them, will be severely judged"
(Even Shelomoh 85, 24).

"Because of this, the spirit of Moshia'h departs and is not coming for the deliverance... When we are not learning this science (Kabbalah) his coming is delayed."
(Commentary of Tikune HaZohar, 81, 92).

Harav Avraham Azulay (grand-father of the 'Hidah) said:
"What was decreed from above; not to study the Kabbalah openly, was for a limited time only, until the end of the year 5260[18]. From there and after, it was allowed, and from the

---

[16] Scholars
[17] Commandment
[18] 1500

year 5300[19] it was decreed that it is a *"Mitsvah"* (commandment) that old and young should study it. For the merit of studying this and for no other merit, the Moshia'h will come.

(Or Ha'Hamah, introduction).

33 *What does the Zohar say about learning the Kabbalah?*

All the souls in this present world, that will make the effort to know their Creator through His secret writings (Kabbalah), will ascend higher than all the other souls that did not learn and understand, and will be first at the time of the resurrection.

(Zohar, Vayeshev, 182, 2)

The man who learns Kabbalah is above all the others.

(Zohar, Shemini, 42, 1)

The one that learns Kabbalah to understand the secrets of the Torah, and the purpose of the *Mistvot*[20] according to the *Sod*[21], is called a "Son" of the Lord.

(Zohar, Vayera).

34 *Why has the study of Kabbalah been discouraged by some?*

All the rabbinical authorities have always agreed on the ultimate importance and truthfulness of the Kabbalah, they

---

[19] 1540
[20] Commandments
[21] Secret

just did not agree on the way this knowledge should be disseminated. Some insisted that only a very selective group should be allowed to learn Kabbalah, and only after attaining a high level of purity and comprehension of all the other writings. Others believed that it should be more accessible and taught to most Jews. During the 16th century with the coming of Shabbetai Tsevi[22] who was called the "Kabbalistic Messiah", the Jewish community was divided between his followers and the "non-believers". After converting to Islam, this false Messiah caused a big deception and mistrust in the teachings of the Kabbalah. The rabbinical authorities of the time became even more severe with the learning of Kabbalah and some were even persecuted for learning or writing on the subject.

35   *Is it not forbidden to study the Kabbalah before the age of forty?*

This decree was canceled about 450 years ago, as it was confirmed and written by Rav Avraham Azulay[23]:

> "What was decreed from above; not to study the Kabbalah openly, was for a limited time only, until the end of the year 5260[24]. From there and after, it was allowed, and from the year 5300[25] it was decreed that it is a *"Mitsvah"* (commandment).   (Or Ha'Hamah, introduction).

---

[22] 1626-1676

[23] The grand-father of the Rav 'Hidah, a respected and accepted authority by all

[24] 1500

[25] 1540

41

Also two of the most important Kabbalists of all times; the Ari Z'al and the Ram'hal started very young as they both died before the age of forty.

36   *Can women study Kabbalah?*

I personally have never seen an interdiction written by the main masters of Kabbalah forbidding women to study Kabbalah. Some even say that women could be more sensitive to understand this knowledge.

37   *Can non-Jews study the Kabbalah?*

Non-Jews that are attracted by the Kabbalah could get an "intellectual" insight of its concepts and a feeling of well-being by its values, but have no direct participation in its realization, since they do not observe its intricate relations with the commandments of the Torah and the prayers. For example; when praying three times a day, we participate in the unification of particular lights or energies for the guidance of the world, by observing the Shabbat this participation is enhanced, and our rituals correspond to very particular actions that are reflected on these energies. About all of the other prayers, rituals or commandments of the Torah are also in direct relation with these lights or energies that are in charge of the guidance, and the manifestation of G-od's presence. This is the reason why throughout the history, all the main and important Kabbalists were very meticulous in observing all the commandments of the Torah in their least details.

38 *Does the learning of the Kabbalah require a certain way of life?*

The serious learning of Kabbalah requires conforming to a way of life where the commandments of the Torah are sincerely observed. A self-discipline, an honest desire to do good with all and to accomplish G-od's will. It is also recommended to seek the guidance of renowned Rabbis that have a strong knowledge of this science.

39 *Why are names of body parts used to describe higher lights?*

In the language of Kabbalah, anthropomorphisms are used only to illustrate the esoteric power of these forces. It is well understood, that there is no physical existence at these higher levels. Thus, when terms such as mouth, ears, or other body parts are used, the intention is to describe the metaphor, or the position they symbolize.

40 *What is the essential knowledge?*

The essential knowledge is the one of the will of the Creator and His ways of guidance in this existence, as explained in the Kabbalah. The other writings explain in the least details "how" to do, but only the Zohar and the Kabbalah explain to us the exact reasons, and effects of all our prayers and actions.

I believe that most yearn to serve at their best the Creator, but have been accustomed to execute and not seek further, or were kept away from this knowledge. It is now time to know and learn and make known this magnificent science, as it is written and recommended[26].

41   *What is the Torah in the Kabbalah?*

The Kabbalah is the mystical and esoteric explanation of the Torah. All the profound secrets explained in the Kabbalah, are alluded in the letters, words and different stories narrated in the Torah.

The Torah contains four levels of comprehension, of which the highest is the *Sod* (secret). At this level, we understand that our *Tefilot* (prayers) and the accomplishment of each one of the *Mitsvot* (commandments), has a direct influence on the superior worlds and on their guidance.

The Torah has 248 positive and 365 negative commandments. Similarly, there are 613 veins and bones to man, 613 parts to the soul, and 613 lights in each *Sephira* or *Partsuf* (configuration), this number is not arbitrary, as there are important interrelations and interactions between them.

Through the knowledge of Kabbalah, we can get to a level of true understanding of the will of the Creator, and in a way "decode" the profound secrets of our holy Torah.

---

[26] See "What the rabbinical authorities have declared about learning the Kabbalah"

42   What is "Ma'ase Bereshit"?

It is the name given for all the details of the beginning of the creation, from the *Tsimtsum*[27], the first worlds, the *Sephirot* etc.

43   What is "Ma'ase HaMerkava"?

It is the name given for all the details of the *Sephirot, Partsufim* - configurations, *Tikunim* - reparation and *Zivugim* - unions that make the guidance.

44   What is the Merkava (heavenly chariot)?

The *Merkava* is the ensemble of the *Partsufim* - configurations *and Sephirot* which make the *Sephirot* trees, with all their inter-relations, actions and illuminations.

45   What is the role of the Hebrew letters (Autiot)?

The *Autiot* are the expression of the *Ma'hshava* (thought). In combination with the *Ta'amim (cantillation)*, *Nekudot* (vowels), *Tagin* (crowns), or with other letters, they transform the higher lights into action. There are twenty two letters and five ending letters. The five ending letters correspond to the *Gevurot* (rigors).

---

[27] Retraction of His light

The creative forces or energies are the different powers in the four letters of the name of G-od ה-ו-ה-י, and the various letters added to make their different spellings. All the emanations are in the order of this name and all the configurations are drawn from these four letters and their different spellings, which are called *Miluyim* (spelling of the letters).

The lights or forces that are clothed in these letters or their combinations, emanate masculine or feminine configurations that make the guidance of the worlds.

46   *How is G-od unique and yet have so many attributes?*

The light of G-od is unique, of equal force, quality and beyond all description. Since the concept of limitlessness is above our human comprehension, we therefore have to use terms accessible to our understanding. In the Kabbalah, the term 'quality' is used, to differentiate the various transformations of this "unique light", and to help us understand its effects upon the guidance of the worlds.

The *Sephirot* or configurations are called the attributes or qualities of G-od. A *Sephira* is in a way a "filter" which transforms this unique light in a particular force or quality, by which the Creator guides the worlds.

47   *Why is G-od called "Ein Sof" (Infinite) in the Kabbalah?*

"Ein Sof" is the Name of G-od that is the most used in the Kabbalah. His light is perfect, and cannot be measured by any definition or limiting terms. If we think about definitions, we introduce a notion of limit, or absence of its opposite. Being ourselves distinct separate beings, we cannot grasp the concept of the "non-distinct". Everything we know is finite, by having a measure or an opposite.

We therefore use the name "*Ein Sof*" (without limit) since we know and admit that G-od and the concept of limitlessness or without end is beyond our human comprehension.

48   *When is the name of G-od; "Elohi-m" used?*

This name denotes rigor in the actions of G-od. It is represented by the *Sephira Gevurah* (rigor).

49   *What is the Zohar?*

The *Zohar* - The book of Splendor, was written by Rabbi Shim'on Bar Yo'hay who lived in Israel during the 2nd century. To escape the Romans, Rabbi Shim'on Bar Yo'hay went into hiding with his son *Rabbi El'azar* in a cave for thirteen years and composed the *Zohar* during this time.

The Zohar is is the esoteric and mystical explanation of the Torah, and the base for most of the Kabbalah writings. It is mostly written in Aramaic and is divided into many sub-chapters of the different portions of the weekly readings of the Torah. Often in metaphors, it deals with all the subjects that make the Jewish mysticism, the details and systems of guidance, the metaphysic, reincarnation etc.

50   *Who is the Ari Z'al?*

Rabbi Its'hak Luria Ashkenazi; the Ari Z'al, was born in Jerusalem in 1534 and became the leading Kabbalist in Tsfat. He explained and clarified all the main concepts of the Kabbalah, and also innovated in the explanation of the *Sephirot* and *Partsufim (configurations)*. He is the author of the corpus '"*Ets 'Haim*"[28] which contains all his works in the style of *Sha'are* (entrances), and is today the major reference in Kabbalah.

---

[28] Tree of life

CREATION

10 Questions

51   *What is the Hishtalshelut – (chain of events)?*

In the Kabbalah, the *Hishtalshelut* is the chain of events starting from the first act of G-od in this creation which is the "*Tsimtsum*" (retraction), followed by the entrance of the *Kav* (ray of His light), the first configurations of the *Sephirot*, the unfolding of the worlds, until the complex arrangements that make the guidance of these worlds.

52   *What is the Tsimtsum - (retraction)?*

In the beginning, there was no existence except His presence, the Creator was alone, occupying all space with His light. His light without end, borders or limit, filled everything. His light being of such holiness and intensity, it is not possible for any being to exist in its proximity.

The "*Tsimtsum (retraction)*" is the first act of the *Ein Sof* (infinite) in the creation. It is the retraction of His light from a certain space and encircling it, so as to reduce its intensity and allow created beings to exist.

By these boundaries, He revealed the concepts of rigor and limit needed by the created beings, and gave a space for all the created to exist.

53   *What is the 'Hallal – (vacant space)?*

It is the space left by the *Tsimtsum* (retraction) of His light. This space is circular and contains all possibilities of existence for separated entities, given that they are distanced from the intensity of His light.

54   *What is the Reshimu - (imprint)?*

When His light retracted forming the round space, a trace of it, called the *Reshimu* (imprint) remained inside the *'Hallal* (vacant space). This lower intensity light, allowed a space of existence (*Makom*[29]), for all the created worlds and beings.

The roots of all future existence and events are in the *Reshimu* (imprint). Nothing can come into existence, without having its root in this imprint, but the Lord still guides all.

55   *What is the Kav – (ray)?*

After the *Tsimtsum* (contraction), a ray of His light entered this empty space.

This straight ray of light called "*Kav*", emerged from the *Ein Sof* (infinite), and entered on one side of the "'*Hallal*" (vacant space). The combination of the *Kav* (ray) and the *Reshimu* (imprint) is what will give existence to the *Sephirot* with which He governs the worlds. The *Kav* is the innermost interiority of all this creation.

56   *Why are the letters of the name of G-od spelled differently?*

All creative forces or energies, originate from the different powers of the four letters of the name of G-od ה-ו-ה-י, and

---

[29] Space – possibility of existence

the various letters added to make their different spellings. Depending on which letters are used, the numerical value of the name changes, and each one of these possibilities becomes different in its nature and actions.

The four spellings are:
- בן ,מה , סג, עב - 'A"V (72), SaG (63), MaH (45), BaN (52)

עב – הי ויו הי יוד   - 'A"V = 72

סג – הי ואו הי יוד   - SaG = 63

מה - הא ואו הא יוד   - MaH = 45

בן – הה וו הה יוד   - BaN = 52

Each name can also be divided and subdivided as:
'A"V of 'A"V, SaG of 'A"V, MaH of 'A"V ...
BaN of BaN of SaG, SaG of MaH of 'A"V etc.

All the emanations and *Sephirot* that came out of *Adam Kadmon* (Primordial man) by way of his apertures were of the various aspects of these four names. They have different actions, and all the *Partsufim* (configurations) will be constructed by their union.

57   *What are the Sephirot of the name of BaN (52)?*

They correspond to the feminine aspect - rigor, and came out from *Adam Kadmon* (Primordial man). When the first three *Sephirot* – KHB (Keter, 'Hokhma, Binah) came out, they were able to stand in three columns, the seven lower *Sephirot* could not stand in this order; they formed a single descending line and broke. This imperfect arrangement and the breaking of these feminine *Sephirot* of the aspect of the name of *BaN*, is the first origin of the *Sitra A'hra*[30] or "evil".

58   *What is the Shvirat HaKelim - breaking of the vessels?*

From the first configuration of *Adam Kadmon* came out different emanations for the construction of the worlds.

From his eyes came out ten *Sephirot* of the aspect of the name of *BaN (52);* corresponding to the feminine aspect - rigor. When they came out, only the first three *Sephirot; Keter, 'Hokhma* and *Binah* received and contained their lights because they were in the three-column arrangement, needed for the direction of Kindness, rigor and mercy, The seven lower *Sephirot* that were not arranged in the three pillar arrangement, could not hold the influx of their lights and broke. To sustain them after they broke, 288 sparks of lights came down as well, because a connection to their original lights was needed to keep them alive.

This caused an important damage called *Shvirat HaKelim* – the breaking of the vessels and it is this imperfect arrangement that is the first origin of the *Sitra A'hra*[31] or "evil". If the seven *Sephirot* had contained their lights, they would not have broken, and the notions of *Kilkul* (damage) and *Tikun* (repair) not existed.

---

[30] Other side – Negative force
[31] Other or negative side

The goal of all the works, deeds and prayers of men in this existence, is to help and participate in the ascent of these 288 sparks to their origin.

With the emanation of other lights, the Creator could have done the *Tikun* (rectification) of all the worlds after the *Shvirat HaKelim (breaking of the vessels),* but then, there would not have been a reason for the participation of man in this *Tikun.* It is to give a possibility to man to act and repair the creation, that G-od restrained in a way his outflow of kindness to this world. At the completion of this *Tikun*[32] of unification between the fallen sparks and their *Sephirot,* it will be the time of the resurrection of the dead and the arrival of *Moshia'h.*

59   *What are the Rapa'h Nitsutsot - (288 Sparks)?*

After the breaking of the *Sephirot*[33], to sustain them, 288 sparks of lights came down as well, because a connection to their original lights was needed to keep them alive. This fall occurred in all the worlds and also in the negative worlds. It is important to understand that all that happens in our world is similar to what occurred in this fall. This separation between a recipient and its light or energy, is the model of the works that have to be accomplished by men in this world, where they have to reunite these sparks with their original recipients by praying and accomplishing the *Mitsvot* – commandments.

---

[32] Rectification
[33] See "Breaking of the vessels"

WORLDS

8 Questions

61   **What is a world?**

A world is a possibility and a type of existence, in a particular dimension. From the first configuration; *Adam Kadmon* (*Primordial man*), emanations made the four lower worlds. There are also negative worlds at the bottom or in contrast, of the positive worlds.

62   **How many worlds are there?**

There are four worlds, their names are:
- *Atsilut* - Emanation
- *Beriah* – Creation
- *Yetsirah* – Formation
- *'Asiah* – Action

63   **What is the difference between these worlds?**

In the first world of *Atsilut* there is no aspect of physical existence, starting from the second world existence of separated entities begin. All the worlds are similar (they all contain 10 *Sephirot* and five configurations), but the quintessence of the higher is superior. There is a screen (divider) that separates one world from another, and from this screen the ten *Sephirot* of the lower world come out.

64   **What is Atsilut?**

The first world to unfold from *Adam Kadmon* (*Primordial man*) is called *Atsilut;* the world of emanation, where there is no existence of the separated, and no *Sitra A'hra (negative force)* even at its lowest levels. It consists of five main *Partsufim* (configurations): *Arikh Anpin, Abah, Imah, Zeir Anpin* and *Nukvah.* One more *Partsuf, 'Atik Yomin,* is on top of them, his three first *Sephirot* are in the superior world (above *Atsilut),* his seven lower *Sephirot* are inside the ten *Sephirot* of *Arikh Anpin,* and make the link with the superior world; *Adam Kadmon* (Primordial man). *Arikh Anpin* reaches from the top to the bottom of *Atsilut.*

From *Atsilut* (emanation) unfolded all the lower worlds, which are the source of existence for the physical worlds, and the possibility of reward, punishment and evil.

65   *What is Beriah?*

The second world after *Atsilut* is *Beriah (creation).* It is the world of the *Neshamot,* of the souls.

66   *What is Yetsirah?*

The third world after *Beriah* is *Yetsirah (formation).* It is the world of spiritual entities, the world of the angels.

67   **What is *'Asiah?***

The fourth world after *Yetsirah* is *'Asiah (action);* the world of action, the world of physical existence. From the last level of the *Sephirot* of *'Asiah - Malkhut* of *'Asiah,* the *Sitra A'hra* (evil) came out.

68   *What are the four types of existence in our world?*

In parallel to the four worlds (*ABYA*), there are four types of existence in our world; mineral corresponding to *'Asiah* (action), vegetal corresponding to *Yetsirah* (formation), animal corresponding to *Beriah* (creation), and man corresponding to *Atsilut* (emanation).

SEPHIROT

20 Questions

69   *What is a Sephira ?*

The light of G-od is unique and of equal force and quality. A *Sephira* is in a way a "filter" which transforms this light in a particular force or attribute, by which the *Ein Sof* (Infinite) directs the worlds.

Each *Sephira* is composed of a vessel called *Keli* (recipient), which holds its part of light called *Or* (light). There is no difference in the *Or* (light) itself; the difference comes from the particularity, or position of the *Sephira*.

70   *How many Sephirot are there and what are their names?*

There are ten *Sephirot,* their names are:

Keter	*Crown*	**Tiferet**	*Beauty*
'Hokhma	*Wisdom*	**Netsa'h**	*Glory*
Binah	*Understanding*	**Hod**	*Splendor*
'Hesed	*Bounty*	**Yesod**	*Foundation*
Gevurah	*Rigor*	**Malkhut**	*Kingship*

There is one more *Sephira* called *Da'at* (Knowledge), which is counted when *Keter* is not.

The first and most important of the *Sephirot* is *Keter*. It is complete kindness to all, even to the not deserving.

The second *Sephira 'Hokhma* is also kindness to all, even to the not deserving, but less than *Keter,* and not always.

65

The third *Sephira Binah* is kindness to all, even to the less deserving, but from her, the rigors start.

The fourth *Sephira 'Hesed* is complete kindness, but to who is deserving.

The fifth *Sephira Gevurah* is full rigor to who is deserving.

The sixth *Sephira Tiferet* is kindness that makes the equilibrium between complete kindness and rigor.

The seventh *Sephira Netsa'h* is diminished kindness to who is deserving.

The eighth *Sephira Hod* is diminished rigor to who is deserving.

The ninth *Sephira* Yesod makes the equilibrium between *Sephira Netsa'h* and *Hod* for the guidance, and is the link or connection between all the superior *Sephirot* and the *Sephira Malkhut.*

The tenth *Sephira* is *Malkhut* translates all the superior emanations into one that is reflected to the creation. It is the link or connection between all the superior *Sephirot* and man.

There are also configurations of one or more *Sephirot* acting in coordination, which are called *Partsufim*.

71   *What is a Sephirotic tree?*

A Sephirotic tree is made of ten *Sephirot* arranged in three columns.

On the right, the *'Hesed* (kindness*)* column: *'Hokhma, 'Hesed, Netsa'h.*
In the middle, the *Ra'hamim* (mercy) column: *Keter, Tiferet, Yesod, Malkhut.*

On the left, the *Din* (rigor) column: *Binah, Gevurah, Hod.*

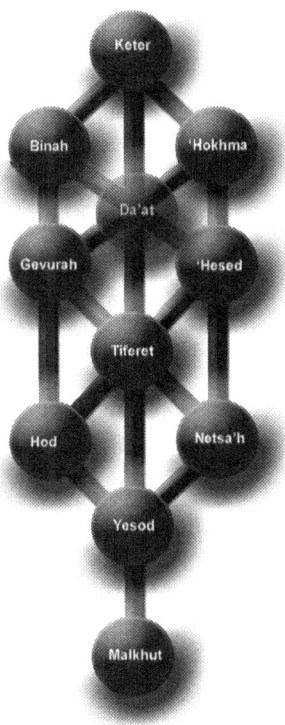

The *Sephira Da'at* is counted when *Keter* is not, also in the *Ra'hamim* column. *Partsufim* (configurations) are also composed of ten *Sephirot* arranged in the same order.

72   *What are the Sephirot Ha'Igulim - (encircling Sephirot)?*

After entering the *'Hallal* (vacant space), the *Kav* (ray) made ten circular *Sephirot*, encircling one another, but still maintained a straight shape. These ten *Sephirot* are in charge of the general guidance of the worlds, and are not influenced by the actions of men.

73   *What are the Sephirot HaYashar - (linear Sephirot)?*

After making the ten circular *Sephirot*, the *Kav* (ray) maintained his straight shape and made ten other *Sephirot*, but this time in a linear arrangement.

They were later arranged in three columns: right, left and middle, representing the guidance of the world in the manner of *'Hesed, Din* and *Ra'hamim* (Kindness, rigor and mercy). This guidance is dependent on time, and the actions of men.

This first configuration of ten *Sephirot* is called *Adam Kadmon* (Primordial Man) and all the other worlds will be formed in the same linear arrangement of Sephirot.

74   *What is Adam Kadmon - (Primordial man)?*

The first configuration, or the first world where the emanated lights were formed into ten *Sephirot* is called *Adam Kadmon* (Primordial Man). It is the union between the *Reshimu* (imprint) and the *Kav* (ray). From this first configuration, all the other worlds came forth into existence, and this first emanation is the origin of all future emanations.

Adam Kadmon being at such close proximity to the *Ein Sof* (Infinite), we cannot grasp anything of its nature. Our understanding only starts from the emanations that came out of him, which are called his branches.

It is from these emanations, that the other four worlds of *Atsilut* (emanation), *Beriah* (creation), *Yetsirah* (formation) and *'Asiah* (action) will unfold.

75   *What are the NeHY?*

Initials of the third triplet of the *Sephirot: Netsa'h, Hod and Yesod.* They mostly act together as the interior guiding force - *Mo'hin* (brains) for a lower *Partsuf* (configuration).

76   *What are the 'HaGaT?*

Initials of the second triplet of the *Sephirot: 'Hesed, Gevurah and Tiferet.* They act together as the second level of the guiding force - *Mo'hin* (brains) for a lower *Partsuf.*

77   *What are the 'HaBaD?*

Initials of the first triplet of the *Sephirot: 'Hokhma, Binah and Da'at.* They act together as the third and higher level of the guiding force - *Mo'hin* (brains) for a lower *Partsuf,* and are called the *Mo'hin* of *Gadlut* (growth).

78   *What is the Sephira Keter - (crown)?*

It is the first and most important of the *Sephirot*.

Its quality is complete kindness to all, even to the not deserving.

Its position is on the top – center of the center column which corresponds to *Ra'hamim* (mercy).

Other *Sephirot* on the same column: *Tiferet, Yesod, Malkhut*.

It makes the *Partsufim - 'Atik Yomin* and *Arikh Anpin*.

Its corresponding name: *AHY-H-* אהי-ה

Its corresponding *Miluy* (spelling) of name: *'A"V -* עב (72), vowel: *Kamatz*

Its physical correspondence: head

Its corresponding level of the soul: *Ye'hidah*

79   *What is the Sephira 'Hokhma - (wisdom)?*

It is the second of the *Sephirot*.

Its quality is Kindness to all, even to the not deserving (but less than *Keter,* and not always).

Its position is on the top - right of the right column which corresponds to *'Hesed* (Kindness).

Other *Sephirot* on the same column: *'Hesed, Netsa'h*.

It makes the *Partsuf Abah* .

Its corresponding name: *YH* י-ה

Its corresponding *Miluy* (spelling) of name: *'A"V -* עב (72), vowel: *Pata'h*

Its physical correspondence: right brain

Its corresponding level of the soul: *'Hayah*

80   *What is the Sephira Binah - (understanding)?*

It is the third of the *Sephirot.*

Its quality is kindness to all, even to the less deserving (but from her, the rigors start).

Its position is on the top - left of the left column which corresponds to *Din* (rigor).

Other *Sephirot* on the same column: *Gevurah, Hod.*

It makes the *Partsuf Imah* .

Its corresponding name: *YHV-H*   י-ה-ו-ה (but with the vowels of *Elokim*)

Its corresponding *Miluy* (spelling) of name: *SaG (63)* - סג, vowel: *Tsere*

Its physical correspondence: left brain

Its corresponding level of the soul: *Neshama*

81   *What is the Sephira Da'at - (Knowledge)?*

It is the fourth of the *Sephirot. Da'at* is counted when *Keter* is not.

Its quality is the guidance that makes the equilibrium between *'Hokhma and Binah.*

Its position is on the center of the center column which corresponds to *'Ra'hamim* (mercy)

Other *Sephirot* on the same column: *Keter, Tiferet, Yesod, Malkhut.*

Its role is mainly to make the *Mo'hin* (brains) for configurations *Z"A* and *Nukvah.*

Its corresponding name: *AHV-H –* אהו-ה

82 *What is the Sephira 'Hesed - (bounty)?*

It is the fourth of the *Sephirot*.
Its quality is complete kindness to who is deserving.
Its position is on the middle – right of the right column which corresponds to *'Hesed* (kindness).
Other *Sephirot* on the same column: *'Hokhma, Netsa'h*.
It is one of the *Sephirot* that make the *Partsuf Z"A*.
Its corresponding name: *El – אל*
Its corresponding *Miluy* (spelling) of name: *MaH* (מה) 45, vowel: *Segol*
Its physical correspondence: right arm
Its corresponding level of the soul: *Rua'h*

83 *What is the Sephira Gevurah - (rigor)?*

It is the fifth of the *Sephirot*.
Its quality is full rigor to who is deserving.
Its position is on the middle – left of the left column which corresponds to *Din* (rigor).
Other *Sephirot* on the same column: *Binah, Hod*.
It is one of the *Sephirot* that make the *Partsuf Z"A*.
Its corresponding name: *Elohi-m   אלהי-ם*
Its corresponding *Miluy* (spelling) of name: *MaH* (מה) 45, vowel: *Sheva*
Its physical correspondence: Left arm
Its corresponding level of the soul: *Rua'h*

84   *What is the Sephira Tiferet - (beauty)?*

It is the sixth of the *Sephirot*.

Its quality is kindness that makes the equilibrium between complete kindness and rigor.

Its position is in the middle of the center column which corresponds to *Ra'hamim* (mercy).

Other *Sephirot* on the same column: *Keter, Yesod, Malkhut*

It is one of the *Sephirot* that make the *Partsuf Z"A*.

Its corresponding name: *YHV-K ה-ו-ה-י*

Its corresponding *Miluy* (spelling) of name: *MaH* (מה) 45, vowel: *'Holam*

Its physical correspondence: body

Its corresponding level of the soul: *Rua'h*

85   *What is the Sephira Netsa'h - (splendor)?*

It is the seventh of the *Sephirot*.

Its quality is diminished kindness to who is deserving.

Its position is on the bottom - right of the right column which corresponds to *'Hesed* (kindness).

Other *Sephirot* on the same column: *'Hokhma, 'Hesed*.

One of the *Sephirot* that make the *Partsuf Z"A*.

Its corresponding name: YKVK *Tsebaot*

צבאות- ה-ו-הי

Its corresponding *Miluy* (spelling) of name: *MaH* (45) (מה), vowel: *'Hirik*

Its physical correspondence: right leg

Its corresponding level of the soul: *Rua'h*

86   *What is the Sephira Hod - (glory)?*

It is the eighth of the *Sephirot*.
Its quality is diminished rigor to who is deserving.
Its position is on the bottom - left of the left column which corresponds to *Din* (rigor).
Other *Sephirot* on the same column: *Binah, Gevurah*.
One of the *Sephirot* that make the *Partsuf Z"A*.
Its corresponding name: *Elohi-m Tsebaot*
אלהי-ם -צבאות
Its corresponding *Miluy* (spelling) of name: *MaH* (45) (מה),
vowel: *Kubutz*
Its physical correspondence: left leg
Its corresponding level of the soul: *Rua'h*

87   *What is the Sephira Yesod - (foundation)?*

It is the ninth of the *Sephirot*.
Its quality is to do the link or connection between all the superior *Sephirot* and *Malkhut*, and the guidance that makes the equilibrium between *Sephira Netsa'h and Hod*.
Its position is on the bottom – center of the center column which corresponds to *Ra'hamim* (mercy).
Other *Sephirot* on the same column: *Keter, Tiferet, Malkhut*
One of the *Sephirot* that make the *Partsuf Z"A*.
Its corresponding name: *Shada- y* -- שד-י
Its corresponding *Miluy* (spelling) of name: *MaH* (45) (מה),
vowel: *Shirik*
Its physical correspondence: masculine organ
Its corresponding level of the soul: *Rua'h*

88   *What is the Sephira Malkhut - (royalty)?*

It is the tenth of the *Sephirot.*

Its quality is to make the guidance that translates all the superior emanations into one, that is reflected to the creation.

Its position is on the bottom – center of the center column which corresponds to *Ra'hamim* (mercy).

Other *Sephirot* on the same column: *Keter, Tiferet, Yesod.*

It makes the *Partsuf Nukvah*, divided in two *Partsufim: Ra'hel* and *Leah*

Its corresponding name: *Adona-y* – אדנ-י

Its corresponding *Miluy* of name: *BaN (52)*- בן, vowel: none

Its physical correspondence: crown on the masculine organ

Its corresponding level of the soul: *Nefesh*

PARTSUFIM

18 Questions

89   *What is a PARTSUF – (configuration)?*

Once the *Sephira* "filters" and transforms the higher light or energy in a particular force or attribute by which the Creator guides the worlds, it can now act alone or with others. *Partsuf* in Aramaic means face, visage or countenance. A face is composed of many and various elements as eyes, nose, mouth, forehead and so on, but all are coordinated as one single unit. A face is unique; it shows the particular identity of a person and is the main vehicle of communication. A *Partsuf* also is a unique configuration of one or more elements (*Sephirot*) acting in coordination like a single unity.

90   **What are the different types of *configurations?***

There are two different types of configurations: masculine and feminine. The masculine bestow kindness, the feminine bestow rigor. The masculine corresponds to *'Hesed* (kindness), the feminine to *Gevurah* (rigor*)*. There are also primary and secondary configurations, which by their union and influence will make the guidance.

91   *What are the actions of a Partsuf?*

The actions and inter-relations of the *Partsufim* are called the *Tikunim* of the *Partsufim* . These *Tikunim* will result in various illuminations and influences of different intensities, depending on time and the actions of man.

The goal of these *Tikunim* is to transmit the lights or energies given to the configurations, once they have been transformed by them or by their unions with others.

The guidance of the world is dependent on the different positioning and interaction of the masculine and feminine *Partsufim*, since they have a direct effect on the measure and balance of the factors of kindness, rigor and mercy.

92   *Do their actions or interactions vary?*

Each day, according to the actions of man, the *Tefilot*[34] during the week, *Shabbat* or *Holidays*, and depending on time, various configurations allow different *Zivugim* (unions) of *Partsufim*, and therefore outflows of abundance of variable intensities.

93   *What are the names of the Partsufim?*

There are five main *Partsufim:*
- *Arikh Anpin*
- *Abah*
- *Imah*
- *Zeir Anpin*
- *Nukvah*

And one on top of them: *'Atik Yomin* (clothed inside *Arikh Anpin*).

Seven other *Partsufim* emerge from these main five.

---

[34] Prayers

94   *From which Sephirot do the Partsufim emerge?*

They emanate from the ten *Sephirot* as follows:

From *Keter:*
- *'Atik Yomin*
- *Arikh Anpin*

From *'Hokhma:*
- *Abah*
- From *Malkhut* of *Abah* - *Israel Saba*
- From *Malkhut* of *Israel Saba* - *Israel Saba* 2

From *Binah:*
- *Imah*
- From *Malkhut* of *Binah* -*Tevunah*
- From *Malkhut* of *Tevunah* - *Tevunah* 2

Israel Saba and *Tevunah* are also called by their initials *ISOT* or *ISOT* 2.

From the six *Sephirot; 'Hesed, Gevurah, Tiferet, Netsa'h, Hod, and Yesod:*
- *Zeir Anpin* also called *Israel*
From *Zeir Anpin* - *Ya'acov*

From *Malkhut:*
- *Nukvah*, divided in two *Partsufim*: *Ra'hel* and *Leah*

95   *What is Partsuf 'Atik Yomin?*

The *Partsuf 'Atik* is superior to all the *Partsufim* (configurations). It has ten *Sephirot*, his aspect of *MaH (45)* corresponds to the masculine principle, his aspect of *BaN (52)* to the feminine, he is called *'Atik* and his *Nukvah*[35]. His *Nukvah* is never separated from him, her back attached to his back, *'Atik* is thus all face; the face of *BaN* corresponding to his back, the face of *MaH* to his front.

96   *What is the role of Partsuf 'Atik Yomin?*

The *Partsuf 'Atik* makes the connection between the worlds, in the world of *Atsilut* (emanation) it is the *Sephira Malkhut* of *Adam Kadmon* (Primordial man) which becomes the *Partsuf 'Atik*. It is the same in the three other worlds of *Beriah* (creation), *Yetsirah* (formation) and *'Asiah* (action), the *Malkhut* of the world above becomes the *Partsuf 'Atik* of the world below.

97   *What is Partsuf Arikh Anpin?*

After *Partsuf 'Atik*, the innermost of all the other *Partsufim* (configurations) is *Arikh Anpin* and his *Nukvah*[36], they make one *Partsuf;* the masculine on the right, and the feminine on the left.

---

[35] Feminine configuration
[36] Feminine configuration

Arikh Anpin is the first *Partsuf* in *Atsilut* (emanation), and the root of all the others which are his branches. *Arikh Anpin* reaches from the top to the bottom of a world.

98   *What are the Partsufim (configurations) Abah and Imah?*

These two *Partsufim (configurations)* are essential in the guidance of the worlds, they are the link between *Partsuf Arikh Anpin* which is the highest configuration, and *Partsuf Zeir Anpin* who communicates these emanations to the worlds by his *Zivug* (union) with the *Partsuf Nukvah*. *Abah* is the *Sephira 'Hokhma, Imah* is the *Sephira Binah*.

99   *What is Partsuf Zeir Anpin?*

Zeir Anpin (Z"A) is composed of the six lower *Sephirot: 'Hesed, Gevurah, Tiferet, Netsa'h, Hod,* and *Yesod*.

It is the main configuration between man and the guidance. At first *Z"A* needs to get his *Mo'hin (directive force),* which are his first three *Sephirot "Hokhma, Binah* and *Da'at* from *Abah* and *Imah,* and to get to a stage of growth. Afterwards, by his unions with the feminine configurations of Ra'hel and Leah will produce the guidance.

100   *What is the role of Partsuf Zeir Anpin?*

For the abundance to come down to the world, *Zeir Anpin* needs to unite with *Nukvah*. There can be abundance only when the masculine and the feminine are in harmony.

Each new day, is of a new emanation that governs it. For each day, there are new *Zivugim* of different aspects of *Z"uN*[37]. The guidance of the world is dependent on the different positioning and interaction, of configurations *Z"A* and *Nukvah*, since they have a direct effect on the measure and balance of the factors of kindness, rigor and mercy. To this effect, the goal of the service of the creatures, is to help prepare the *Partsufim (configurations) Z"A* and *Nukvah* for the *Zivug (union)*, and this by the elevation and adhesion of the worlds by way of the *Tefilot*[38] and observing the *Mitsvot*[39].

101   *What is Partsuf Nukvah ?*

The *Partsuf* (configuration) *Nukvah* represents the feminine – the principle of receiving. It comprises of two distinct *Partsufim*: *Ra'hel* and *Leah*.

The masculine *Partsuf Zeir Anpin* and the feminine *Nukvah,* are the root of all the created. It is by them, that the guidance is manifested.

There is perfection for the masculine only when it completes itself with its feminine, and there can be abundance only when the masculine and the feminine are in harmony. This

---

[37] *Zeir Anpin* and *Nukvah.*
[38] Prayers
[39] Commandments

abundance comes down to the world, by the various *Zivugim* (unions) of *Zeir Anpin* with *Nukvah*.

There are two conditions needed for the *Zivug* (union) to be possible: the *Partsufim* have to be constructed, and the feminine has to stimulate a reaction from the masculine. This stimulation happens because of the *Tikunim* (rectifications) realized by men with the *Tefilot* (prayers) and *Mitsvot*.

102   What is the role of Partsuf Nukvah?

The *Partsuf Nukvah* is the link between the higher *Sephirot* and configurations and the lower beings. She transmits from high the results of the different *Zivugim*[40], since the abundance first comes to Z"A, then to *Nukvah,* and from her, to the lower worlds.

103   What are the Mo'hin (brains) of a configuration?

The *Mo'hin* are the directive force given to a *Partsuf* (configuration) by the configuration above him. There are interior and encircling *Mo'hin*. The interior *Mo'hin* are the *Sephirot NHY (Netsa'h, Hod, Yesod)* of the superior *Partsuf* that enter inside the lower *Partsuf* to be his brains or intelligence. The encircling *Mo'hin* stand on the outside. A *Partsuf* – configuration is not independent and can not act before receiving his directive forces.

---

[40] Unions

104 *What is a Zivug - (union)?*

The *Zivug* is the union of the masculine configuration with its feminine. All the outcomes of the higher emanations are a result of the different unions of the masculine and feminine lights.

For the abundance to come down to the world, the masculine configuration *Zeir Anpin* needs to unite with the feminine configuration *Nukvah (Ra'hel or Leah)*. There can be abundance only when the masculine and the feminine are in harmony. These unions which are influenced by the acts of men and by time, have different effects and will result in various outflows of abundance.

105 *What are the different types of Zivugim?*

The guidance of the world is dependent on the different positioning and interaction, of these masculine and feminine *Partsufim*, since they have a direct effect on the measure and balance of the factors of kindness, rigor and mercy.

Each new day, is of a new emanation that governs it. For each day, there are new *Zivugim* of different aspects of the masculine and feminine configurations.

The different types of unions are the ones between the masculine *Partsufim* called *Zeir Anpin, Israel,* and *Ya'acov* and the feminine configurations called *Nukvah, Ra'hel* and Leah. The goal of the service of the creatures is to help prepare these for these unions, and this, by the elevation and adhesion of the worlds by way of the *Tefilot*[41] and *Mitsvot*[42].

106 *What are the different positions of the configurations?*

There is a notion of closeness and interaction, depending on whether the *Partsufim* face or turn their back to each other. The three possibilities are: face to face, back to face, or back to back.

Face to face is the ideal level and corresponds to the bestowing of abundance.

Back to face denotes a readiness to get close from one side only. It is a position of waiting or longing for the ideal face to face situation.

Back to back is the lowest level, and corresponds to dissimulation and rigor.

The outflows of rigor, goodness and abundance are dependent on the different positioning and interaction of these masculine and feminine *Partsufim*.

---

[41] Prayers
[42] Commandments

GUIDANCE

8 Questions

107   *What are the types of guidance?*

There are two main types of guidance:
- The general guidance, which is for the subsistence of the worlds and nature, is not influenced by the actions of men. This guidance is by the encircling *Sephirot.*

- The variable guidance, which is on the basis of justice, reward and punishment, is dependant on the actions of men. This guidance is by the linear *Sephirot.*

108   *By which attributes or qualities is the guidance manifested?*

The guidance is manifested by the linear *Sephirot* which are arranged in three columns: right, left and middle, representing the guidance of the world in the manner of *'Hesed*, *Din* and *Ra'hamim* - Kindness, rigor and mercy. Some configurations are masculine and bestow kindness, others are feminine and bestow rigor. By their union, different equilibriums of the two forces of Kindness and rigor make the guidance.

109   **What is the attribute of Kindness?**

There are particular moments, or days of bounty during the year, as the Shabbat and Holidays, depending on the different position of the configurations. When the masculine and feminine configurations are face to face it is the ideal level and corresponds to the bestowing of abundance. In the attribute of bounty, the guidance is from the right pillar – the pillar of kindness.

Kindness is mostly manifested by all the masculine aspects of the configurations, the Sephira 'Hesed[43], by the concealments of the aspects of rigor and by the illuminations of the higher lights.

110   *What is the attribute of Judgment?*

There are particular moments, or days of rigor during the year. This is dependent on the different position of the configurations. In the absence of *Zivug* (union) when the masculine and feminine configurations are back to back, it corresponds to dissimulation and rigor. In the attribute of judgment, the guidance is from the left pillar – the pillar of rigor.

Rigor is mostly manifested by all the feminine aspects as: the name of *BaN (52)*, the *Sephira Gevurah* and by all the concealments of the masculine aspects which represent bounty.

111   *What is the attribute of mercy?*

In the attribute of mercy the guidance is from the middle pillar – the pillar of *Ra'hamim* (mercy). This guidance makes the balance between the guidance of rigor and bounty.

---

[43] Bounty

112   *How is the Guidance manifested?*

The Kabbalah explains in details the systems that are put in place for the true guidance of the world, so that we may understand His will. It teaches us that the world is guided by an extremely complex system of forces or lights, which through their interactions provoke chain reactions that impact directly on man and the guidance of the worlds.

The guidance of the worlds is done through the influence of the different *Sephirot* and *Partsufim* (configurations). It is dependent on the different positioning and interactions of all these masculine and feminine configurations, since they have a direct effect on the measure and balance of the factors of kindness, rigor and mercy. The masculine *Partsufim* bestow kindness, the feminine bestow rigor. It is by their unions, that different equilibriums of the two forces of kindness and rigor make the guidance.

113   *What is the will to bestow?*

The will of the Creator is to bestow goodness on His creatures, all the levels of creation were put in place so His kindness could emanate to them, yet in such a way that they would be able to receive it. Free choice and evil were created to give man a possibility of merit when he will choose good over bad, this is in itself a great kindness given to man.

114   *What is the "desire to receive"?*

By his nature, man is himself a *Keli* (recipient) with a will to receive without limits, and containing a spiritual light; his soul. A guidance based on this desire will permit anything without restriction, and not allow man to have merit.

The perfect goal for man is to elevate his bodily desires by sanctifying his ways, and resemble his Creator by becoming a giver with a will to bestow goodness to all.

MITSVOT

3 Questions

115   What are the Mitsvot (commandments) in the Kabbalah?

The Torah contains four levels of comprehension, of which the highest is the Sod (secret). At this level, we understand that the accomplishment of each one of the Mitsvot (commandments) has a direct influence on the superior worlds and on their guidance.

The Kabbalah teaches us these complex systems of forces or lights that affect the guidance, their various interactions and their numerous ramifications, and how they are affected by the accomplishment of the Mitsvot[44].

116   What is the relation between the Mitsvot and the Sephirot?

As there are 613 parts to each Sephira and Partsuf, 613 veins and bones to man, and 613 parts to the soul, there are also 613 Mitsvot. This number is not arbitrary as there are important interrelations and interactions between them.

By accomplishing the Mitsvot and the Tefilot (prayers), men do the necessary Tikunim (rectifications) to detach and eliminate the Klipot (husks) which are the manifestation of the negative force that obstruct the lights of the Sephirot, conceal man from his root and from the light.

---

[44] Commandments

117 *What is the goal of the Mitsvot?*

The goal of all the *Mitsvot*, deeds and prayers is to help and participate in the various unions of the configurations, and the ascent of the fallen 288 sparks to their origin, in order for man to make the *Tikun* of his soul and of the world.

The goal of the accomplishment of the *Mitsvot* are:
- To reinforce and purify man
- To act on and influence the guidance
- To help accomplish the *Tikun* of the creation

PRAYER

9 Questions

118 *What is a Tefilah (prayer)?*

A prayer is a ritual composed of particular words and parts of sacred writings, to help and participate in the unification of the superior lights *(Partsufim)* for an outflow of abundance and for the guidance of the world. The order of the *Tefilot* (prayers) is based on the systems of ascension of the worlds, as explained in the Kabbalah.

At this level of comprehension, we understand that our *Tefilot*[45] have a direct influence on the superior worlds and on their guidance. When one understands the systems and actions of the *Tefilot,* he realizes the importance of our rituals, because only man, by praying and the accomplishment of the *Mitsvot* (commandments), can influence these very powerful forces.

119 *Why do we have to pray everyday?*

Each new day, is of a new emanation that governs it and has its own identification and role. For each day, there are new *Zivugim* (unions) of different aspects of the masculine and feminine *Partsufim* (configurations).

A full day is divided in two; day and night, and each half is again divided in two (dawn and day, dusk and night). For each part, there is a *Tefilah*[46], for the two parts of day: *Sha'hrit* and *Min'ha,* for the two parts of nights: *'Arvit* and

---

[45] Prayers
[46] Prayer

Tikun 'Hatsot. Therefore, each prayer has a precise and well define role, in a particular and unique moment.

120   *What is the role of the prayers?*

For the abundance to come down to the world, the masculine *Partsuf* (configuration) *Zeir Anpin* needs to unite with the feminine configuration *Nukvah*. There can be outflows from high only when the masculine and the feminine are in harmony. During the week, *Shabbat* or Holidays, and depending on time, each prayer has its own role in influencing the various configurations to allow different *Zivugim* (unions), and therefore outflows of abundance of variable intensities.

Starting from the first sentence of *Mode Ani*[47], recited when opening our eyes, until the end of the morning prayer, there is a constant elevation and adhesion of the worlds of *'Asiah* (action), *Yetsirah (formation)* and *Beriah (creation)* to the world of *Atsilut (emanation)*, to finally realize this *Zivug (union)* of the masculine and feminine configurations and to receive the results of these unions, which are kindness, mercy, peace etc.

121   *What is the goal of the different blessings?*

When saying the blessing with the Kabbalistic meditation on the appropriate words or names, we act and participate directly on the *Tikun* (repair) of the thing being blessed, or

---

[47] Thanking G-od for giving us back our soul

trigger an action on high in the different *Sephirot* or configurations.

122   *Why do we do a blessing before, and after eating something?*

If a soul has been reincarnated in a fruit or in an other type of food, by doing the blessing we do the *Tikun* (repair) of this soul and liberate it to ascend to its origin.

123   *What is a Hekhal - (portal)?*

In each world there are seven *Hekhalot* (portals). Their role is to allow the adhesion and attachment of the different levels of a world to the next.

Their principal function is the ascension of the *Tefilot* (prayers) until the seventh highest *Hekhal (portal) Kodesh Hakodashim.*

124   *What are the names and the correspondence of the Hekhalot (portals)?*

	Hekhal / Portal	Corresponding to
First	Livnat Hasapir	Yesod and Malkhut
Second	'Etsem Hashamayim	Hod
Third	Nogah	Netsa'h
Fourth	Zekhut	Gevurah
Fifth	Ahavah	'Hesed
Sixth	Ratson	Tiferet
Seventh	Kodesh Kodashim	Keter, 'Hokhma and Binah

125   *What is "Kavanah" - (concentration – intention)?*

There are different levels of *Kavanah*. The basic *Kavanah* is to understand the words, and concentrate on the intention of the blessing or the *Tefilah* (prayer). The higher level is to meditate on the different systems of permutation of names and *Partsufim* (configurations), to get a particular action or result. About each word and part of the prayer has a role or a precise action in the union of the configurations.

126   *What is the goal of the Kavanot?*

The order of the *Tefilot* is based on the systems of ascension of the worlds as explained in the Kabbalah. At this level, we understand that our *Tefilot* have a direct influence on the superior worlds and on their guidance.

Starting from the first act in the morning of *Netilat Yadayim* (washing of the hands three times in alternation), until the end of the *Tefilah*, there is a constant elevation for a precise goal.

The *Hekhalot* (portals) are the different levels of ascension of the *Tefilot* before reaching the seventh highest *Hekhal* (portal), *Kodesh Hakodashim*. Their principal function is to allow the adhesion and attachment to a next dimension according to a well define and organized system.. During the *Tefilot*, he who knows the system of ascension of the *Hekhalot* (portals), concentrates on the words where are hinted the precise action of the *Hekhal (portal)*. He aims to help in the realization of the particular *Zivug* (union) of the *Tefilah*.

When one understands the systems and actions of the prayers, he realizes the importance of our rituals, which are rather dynamic and have the power to act and influence from here to the higher worlds.

TIKUN

9 Questions

127   *What is a Tikun – (rectification – action)?*

In Hebrew, the word "*Tikun*" has different meanings. It can be understood as reparation or rectification, and also as function, relation or action.

There are different types of *Tikunim:*
- *Tikunim* that took place in the first emanations to repair the worlds.
- *Tikunim* for the construction and inter-relations of the *Sephirot* and *Partsufim* (configurations).
- *Tikunim* of certain *Partsufim* (function or action) for the guidance of the worlds.
- *Tikunim* (rectifications) for the souls.

128   *What was the first Tikun to repair the worlds?*

After the *Shvirat HaKelim* (breaking of the vessels), the first *Tikun* was the union of the *Sephirot* of MaH *(45)* and BaN *(52)* in complex arrangements, as to allow the feminine BaN to be repaired by the masculine *MaH,* and for the *Sephirot* to stand in the three-column arrangement for the guidance of kindness, rigor and mercy.

129   *How were the broken Sephirot repaired?*

At first, a drawing force made the broken recipients of the *Sephirot* of BaN ascend to their lights, after falling in the lower worlds. Then, from a new emanation emerged masculine *Sephirot* of the aspect of the name of MaH *(45)* (mercy) to unite with the feminine *Sephirot* of BaN *(52)* (rigor). It is by this union that new repaired configurations emerged constructed now by both these aspects.

130 *How are the Tikunim of the configurations realized?*

The *Tikunim* (construction - inter-relations) of the *Partsufim* masculine and feminine are achieved by way of *Zivug* (union) of the superior configurations that will give birth to a lower one. The *Tikunim* of interdependence are realized by different projected illuminations between the configurations, or by the dressing of a configuration in an other.

131 **What are the *Tikunim* of the *Partsufim* for the guidance?**

For the guidance, the *Tikunim* of the *Partsufim* (configurations) are their actions, illuminations and inter-relations to influence the worlds, and for the ascent of the fallen sparks of lights. Some configurations change in size or power, and reinforce to accentuate their influence on the *Sephirot,* depending on time and the actions of man.

132 **What is a *Tikun* for a soul?**

The *Tikun* (reparation) of a soul is realized by the reincarnation. By accomplishing what he did not accomplish, or repairing what needed repair, man makes the necessary *Tikun* of his soul which can now elevate to the higher realms and rejoin its source. If man does not do the *Tikun* of the level of his soul for which he came, he comes back and reincarnates[48].

133   What is *Tikun 'Olam* – general *Tikun?*

It is the final goal of this existence, the harmony between the creatures and their Creator, and in the creation itself. All the fallen sparks ascend to their source, evil and suffering do not exist anymore. By giving man a role in the general *Tikun* (*Tikun 'Olam*), it is now up to him to restore, and make the necessary reparations to the world. However, if man does not act accordingly, the *Tikun* will still be realized, but in the time set by the Creator.

134   How do we participate in the ascent of the 288 sparks?

The goal of all the works, deeds and prayers of men in this existence, is to help and participate in the ascent of the 288 fallen sparks[49] to their origin. Each *Mitsva*[50] or *Tephila*[51] corresponds to a particular action in the *Tikun*[52] of this damage and the ascent of the sparks of lights. The *Tefilot*[53] are build as a very precise system to help this elevation and attachment.

---

[48] See *Gilgul*
[49] See "What are the Rapa'h Netsutsot – 288 sparks"
[50] Commandment
[51] Prayer
[52] Repair
[53] Prayers

135 *What is the final goal of the reunification of the sparks?*

At the completion of this *Tikun*[54] of unification between the fallen sparks and their *Keli*[55], when the damage of the breaking of the vessels will be completely repaired, it will be the time of the resurrection of the dead and the arrival of *Moshia'h*.

---

[54] Rectification
[55] Recipient

SOULS

5 Questions

136   What is the soul in the Kabbalah?

The soul is the spiritual entity inside the body, the latter being only his outer garment. The soul comes down from the world of *Beriah* (creation) and enters the body for a limited time, before rejoining again its origin.

It has five names: *Nefesh*, *Rua'h*, *Neshama*, *'Hayah* and *Ye'hidah*, which correspond to its five different levels.

137   Are there different "qualities" of souls?

Each soul has its origin in the different worlds and *Partsufim*. The quality of the soul will depend from which *Partsuf* and from which world it has its root. A soul with a higher origin, will be of superior quality and will have a better potential of understanding and getting closer to its Creator.

138   What are the different roots of the souls?

Since it is men that provoke the union of the four worlds, it is necessary for their souls to have their origin from them and from the five *Partsufim*:

Soul	Partsuf	World
Nefesh	Nukvah	'Asiah
Rua'h	Zeir Anpin	Yetsirah
Neshama	Imah	Beriah
'Hayah	Abah	Atsilut
Ye'hidah	Arikh Anpin	Atsilut

115

Each level of the soul is subdivided in five levels. As for the level of *Nefesh* there are:

- *Nefesh* of *Nefesh*
- *Rua'h* of *Nefesh*
- *Neshama* of *Nefesh*
- *'Hayah* of *Nefesh*
- *Ye'hidah* of *Nefesh*

Each one of these levels of the soul subdivides for each level of *Partsuf* and for each world. Therefore, there are five levels of the souls for *Partsuf Nukvah* and there are five levels of *Partsufim* for the world of *'Asiah* etc. Also, as there are in each world ten *Sephirot*, each soul has its origin corresponding to one of them.

139   *How are the higher levels of the souls acquired?*

The higher levels of the soul cannot be acquired at once. Most men only have the level of *Nefesh,* and if they merit, they will acquire the next levels - but one by one.

To reach the next higher level of his soul, man must do the *Tikun* (repair) of all the preceding levels. To acquire his level of *Neshama*, he must do the *Tikun* of all the levels of the *Sephirot* and *Partsufim*[56] of his *Nefesh* and *Rua'h* etc.

---

[56] Configurations

140   *What are the different levels of the soul?*

Nefesh is the first and lower level. It is acquired at birth and before the next levels.

Rua'h is the second level and is acquired before the next levels.

Neshama is the third level and can be acquired only after acquiring the level of *Nefesh* and *Rua'h*.

'Hayah is the fourth level and can only be acquired after the preceding levels.

Ye'hidah is the fifth land higher level; it is very rarely attained and can only be acquired after the *Tikun* (rectification) of all the preceding levels.

REINCARNATION

7 Questions

141   *Does reincarnation exist?*

The Kabbalah explains in details the different systems of reincarnation of the souls. In his book "Sha'are Haguilgulim"[57], the Ari Z'al gives the origin and the different reincarnations of most of the important biblical figures.

142   *What is a Gilgul (reincarnation)?*

The *Tikun* (rectification) of the soul is realized by the *Gilgul* (reincarnation), and by the *'Ibur* (attachment). The *Gilgul* is the reincarnation of a soul from the time of birth until death, the *'Ibur* is an attachment of another soul to his, which could come and leave anytime. Once the soul leaves the body, if it did not accomplish what it came for, it ascends and waits to return in a new body for a chance to do its Tikun.

It is only by accomplishing this lack or shortcoming that the soul will realize its *Tikun* and elevate to the higher realms to rejoin its source.

143   *What is a 'Ibur (attachment of a soul)?*

To help him accomplish a particular act, or the missing *Mitsvot*[58], another soul could attach to his soul (*'Ibur*), until he accomplishes it, and then departs. The missing *Mitsva*

---

[57] Gates of Reincarnations
[58] Commandments of the Torah

could be one he chose not to do, or one he could not do in his previous life.

144   *How many time can a soul reincarnate?*

As long as one undertakes the *Tikun*[59] of his soul in three reincarnations, he will come back again and reincarnate as needed to complete his *Tikun*. However, if he maintains his wrong behavior, he will not come back after the third reincarnation.

145   *Why does a soul need to reincarnate?*

The goal of all the complex systems of reincarnation has only one purpose: to allow man to merit by his own efforts, to get closer to his Creator by perfecting his ways and doing the *Tikun* of his soul. By reincarnating, it is given to the soul one more chance to do its final *Tikun*.

146   *Can a soul reincarnate in an other form?*

It could reincarnate in one of the four types of existence in our world: mineral, vegetal, animal, and man.

---

[59] Rectification - repair

147 *Will there be resurrection of the dead?*

The resurrection of the dead is the final goal of the six thousand years. When a man dies and his soul separates from his body, the latter will remain with a spark of energy or light, to allow the conservation of the body from the time the soul has left him, until the resurrection.

NEGATIVE FORCE

5 Questions

148   *What is the Sitra A'hra – (negative force)?*

The breaking of the vessels caused a descent of all the worlds. The fourth world *'Asiah,* fell even lower, and from its end, the *Sitra A'hra* or evil came out.

The *Sephirot* have their origin in the *Kedushah* (Holiness) of the Infinite, but this opposite type of existence[60] could not come to be from a perfect source; it had to originate from a defective state. Its root is in the lack, or absence of the *Kedushah*. These *Klipot* (husks) obstruct the lights of the *Sephirot*, conceal man from his root and from the light.

In parallel (opposite) to the four positive worlds, this negative entity - *Sitra A'hra,* also has its four worlds, with its ten groups of negative angels. These husks nourish from the extremities of the higher lights, when the latter are weakened by the bad deeds of the lower beings. As a result, the destructive angels get more powers and come to do evil in the world.

149   *Why is there a "Negative force"?*

The existence of the "Negative force" was willed by the Creator to give man free will. With falsehood, it almost constantly tries to seduce him, and make him stumble. To acquire merit, man must constantly try to overcome his bad impulse and do good.

---

[60] Negative force

150   How does the "Negative force" get strength?

The good deeds of man have an effect on the four higher worlds, his bad deeds; on the four lower worlds. It is only when man sins, that the negative force can grow in strength and do more harm in the world. When men act negatively, they cause a deterioration that reach the lower worlds and give strength to the *Klipot*[61] to attach and nourish from the *Sephirot* of the higher worlds.

Similarly, inside of man, this negative aspect that grows in him, is his *Yetser Hara'* (negative impulse)*,* it cuts him off from the higher worlds, and uproots him from the *Kedushah*[62].

151   What are the Klipot - (husks)?

The *Klipot* are the manifestation of the negative force. They obstruct the lights of the *Sephirot,* and conceal man from his root and from the light. Because of the bad deeds of the lower beings, the *Klipot* get their strength and do evil in the world by attaching to the higher lights.

152   What are the different levels of Klipot?

There are four main levels of *Klipot.* They correspond to the four lower worlds, which also comprise of *Sephirot* and configurations as in the positive worlds.

---

[61] Husks
[62] Holiness

ANGELS

6 Questions

153   *What is an angel?*

An angel is a spiritual entity created for a specific purpose. It has no free choice and acts according to the will of the Creator.The world of the angels is the third world; '*Olam Yetsirah* - the world of formation.

154   *What are the different types of angels?*

There are two types of angels: the angels of the nature who were created at the beginning of the world, they are in charge of the nature itself. The second types are the angels of "reward and punishment". They accomplish the will of the divine light inside the *Sephirot,* and are renewed constantly depending on the deeds of men.

155   *How many groups of angels are there?*

The angels of peace make ten groups and serve the *Sephirot* of the positive world, while the angels of destruction make ten levels and serve the *Sephirot* from the lower opposite world.

The ten groups of positive angels are divided as follows: three groups in the world of *Beriah* (creation), six groups in the world of *Yetsirah* (formation), and one group in the world of '*Asiah* (action).

156   *Are there negative angels?*

The other entity, which is called the *Sitra A'hra* – (the other side, or the negative force) has its own angels, as in the positive world, but of a lower force. Its destructive angels subdivide in the same order as well, depending on their importance they are from its own worlds of *Beriah*, *Yetsirah* or *'Asiah*.

157   *Do angels have free choice?*

Angels only have the *Yester Tov* – good impulse, and most are created for one mission.

158   *Are men superior to angels?*

Men are considered superior to angels because the origin of their souls is from a higher world. The fact that only men have free choice to do good or bad gives them a merit[63] that angels do not have.

---

[63] If they do good

GEMATRIA

2 Questions

159   ***What is Gematria?***

Gematria or Numerology is the addition of the numerical values of the letters of words. Each Hebrew letter has its own numerical value, and the fact that some words have the same numerical value is not just coincidence, but denotes a similarity or complementarity. Hidden or secret meanings are hinted in the mathematical total of words, or by using different systems of *Gematriot*.

160   ***How many types of different Gematriot are there?***

There are seven main types of *Gematriot*:
- *Ragil*
- *Katan*
- *HaKlali*
- *Kolel*
- *HaKadmi*
- *HaPerati*
- *Miluy*

1 - *Ragil*: the numbers of the letters are as follows:

From	To	Value
א	ט	1 - 9
י	צ	10 -90
ק	ת	100 - 400
ך	ץ	500 -900

Ex :   הארץ   = 1106

2 – *Katan*: tens and hundreds are reduced to one digit.

From	To	Value
א	ט	1 - 9
י	צ	1 - 9
ק	ת	1 - 4
ך	ץ	5 -9

Ex :   הארץ = 17

3 – *HaKlali*: the *Ragil* value of the word squared.

Ex : הארץ = 1106 * 1106 = 1 223 236

4 – *Kolel*: the *Ragil* value of the word + the numbers of letters, or + 1 for the word.

Ex : הארץ   = 1106 + 4 = 1110 or 1106 + 1 = 1107

5 – *HaKadmi* : each letter has its *Ragil* value plus the total of all the ones preceding it.

From	To	Value
א	ט	1 - 45
י	צ	55 – 495
ק	ת	595 –1495
ך	ץ	1995 – 4995

Ex : הארץ = 15+1+795+4995 = 5806

6 – *HaPerati* : each letter is squared.

Ex : הארץ = 5 * 5 = 25, 1 * 1 = 1
200 * 200 = 40 000, 900 * 900 = 810 000 Total = 850 026

7 – *Miluy:* the sum of the spelling of each letter.

Letter	Miluy	Value
ה	הא	6
א	אלף	111
ר	ריש	510
ץ	צדי	104

Ex : הארץ = 731

By the *Gematriot*, we see that each letter and word has a dynamic meaning beyond the simple definitions. Gematria is only one of the secret ways of interpreting the hidden meanings in the Torah.

Transliteration of the letters

Letter	Name	Equivalent	Transliteration
א	Aleph	A, O, E, I	A, O, E, I
ב	Beit	B, V	B, V
ג	Gimel	G	G
ד	Dalet	D	D
ה	He	H	H
ו	Vav	V	V
ז	Zain	Z	Z
ח	'het		'h
ט	Tet	T	T
י	Yud	Y	Y
כ	Khaf	C, K, KH	C, K, KH
ל	Lamed	L	L
מ	Mem	M	M
נ	Nun	N	N
ס	Samekh	S	S
ע	'ain		'
פ	Pey	P, F	P, F
צ	Tsadey	TS	TS
ק	Kuf	C, K	C, K
ר	Resh	R	R
ש	Shin	S, SH	S, SH
ת	Tav	T	T

139

GLOSSARY

א"ק
A"K
Adam Kadmon
Initials

אבא
Abah
Partsuf Abah
One of the five main *Partsufim* (configurations). It is the *Sephira 'Hokhma*.

אבא ואמא
Abah ve Imah
Partsufim Abah and Imah
These two *Partsufim (configurations)* are essential for the guidance of the worlds, *Abah* is the *Sephira 'Hokhma, Imah* is the *Sephira Binah*.

אבחנה
Av'hana
Distinction – Insight
Understanding of the deeper meaning or Kabbalistic interpretation.

אבר
Ever
Organ – Limb (Anthropomorphism)
In the language of Kabbalah, anthropomorphisms are used only to illustrate the esoteric power of these forces.

אדם קדמון
Adam Kadmon
Primordial man - World on top of Atsilut
This first configuration, or the first world where the emanated lights were formed into ten *Sephirot*.

אדנ-י
Adona-y
One of the names of G-od, represented by the *Sephira Malkhut.*

אהי-ה
AHY-H
One of the names of G-od, represented by the *Sephira Keter.*

אור
Or
Light
Term used to describe an emanation, a force or energy.

אחור
A'hor
Backside – Behind
In general it represents rigor.

אחר
A'her
Other
Name also used for the other side or negative force.

אילן
Ilan
Tree
The disposition of the *Sephirot* in the three pillars arrangement is called the *Sephirotic* tree.

אין סוף
Ein Sof
The without end or limit – Infinite
One of the names of G-od.
The Name of G-od that is the most used in the Kabbalah.

אלוה-ים
Elohi-m
One of the names of G-od, represented by the *Sephira Gevurah.* In general it denotes rigor in the actions of G-od.

אמא
Imah
Partsuf Imah
One of the five main configurations. It is the *Sephira Binah.*

אצילות
Atsilut
World of Emanation
It is the highest of the four worlds, on top of the worlds of *Beriah, Yetsirah* and *'Asiah.* From *Atsilut* unfolded all the lower worlds, which are the source of existence for the physical worlds.

אצילות בריאה יצירה עשייה
Atsilut, Beriah, Yetsirah and 'Asiah

From the first configuration; *Adam Kadmon* (*Primordial man*) emanations made the four lower worlds.

The first world is *Atsilut* – the world of emanation. Under the divider of *Atsilut* is the world of *Beriah* (creation) - the world of the *Neshamot* (souls). Under the divider of *Beriah* is the world of *Yetsirah* (formation) - the world of the angels. Under the divider of *Yetsirah* is the world of *'Asiah* (action) - the physical world.

ארי ז"ל
Ari Z'al

Rabbi Its'hak Luria Ashkenazi
Born in Jerusalem in 1534, died in 1572 in Tsfat, Israel.
He was the leading Kabbalist in Tsfat, he explained and clarified all the main concepts of the Kabbalah. He is the author of the "Ets 'Haim".

אריך אנפין
Arikh Anpin

Partsuf – Long countenance
It is the main *Partsuf* (configuration) in each world. All the other *Partsufim* are his "branches".

אתב"ש
ATBaSH

Permutation of letters to understand hidden meanings of words. First letter replaced by the last, second by the before last etc.

ב"ן
BaN (52)
Miluy (spelling) of the name י-ה-ו-ה with a total of 52
It corresponds to the feminine aspect - rigor,

בינה
Binah
Sephira (understanding)
Third of the *Sephirot*.

ברוך הוא
Barukh Hu, or B'H
Blessed He is
Used after the pronunciation or writing of G-od's names.

בריאה
Beriah
World of creation – of the souls
The second world to unfold is called *Beriah*; the world of creation. It is the world of the *Neshamot* (souls). It is under *Atsilut* and on top of *Yetsirah* and *'Asiah*.

בר יוחאי
Bar Yo'hay
Rabbi Shim'on Bar Yo'hay
To escape the Romans he went into hiding with his son Rabbi El'azar in a cave for thirteen years and composed the Zohar.

ברכה
Berakhah
Blessing

When saying the blessing with the Kabbalistic meditation on the appropriate words or names, we act and participate directly on the *Tikun* (repair) of the thing being blessed.

ג' ראשונות
Shalosh Rishonot
The three first Sephirot
Keter, 'Hokhma, Binah

ג"ר
G"aR
The three first Sephirot
Keter, 'Hokhma, Binah

גבול
Gevul
Boundary – Limit

By putting boundaries to His light, the Creator revealed the concepts of rigor and limit needed by the created beings, and gave a space for all the created to exist.

גבורה
Gevurah
Rigor

The outcome of His light, once filtered by the *Sephira Gevurah* emanates rigor.
Rigor is mostly manifested by all the feminine

aspects as: the name of *BaN (52)*, the *Sephira Gevurah* and by all the concealments of the masculine aspects which represent bounty.

גבורה

Gevurah

Sephira (Rigor)

Fifth of the *Sephirot.*

גימטריה

Gematria

Numerical values of the letters

Each letter has its own numerical value. The fact that some words have the same numerical value is not just coincidence, but denotes a similarity or complementarity.

גלגול

Gilgul

Reincarnation

The *Tikun* of the soul is realized by the *Gilgul* (reincarnation), and by the *'Ibur* (attachment). The *Gilgul* is the reincarnation of a soul from the time of birth until death.

גן עדן

Gan 'Eden

The Garden of Eden

The place of rest for the *Neshamot* (souls) after their separation with their former physical bodies. There is a lower and a higher *Gan 'Eden.*

גן עדן עליון
Gan 'Eden 'Elyon
The upper Garden of Eden
In the higher *Gan 'Eden*, the *Neshamot* (souls) are enjoying pure spiritual pleasures, and do not have any spiritual image resembling their former bodies.

גן עדן תחתון
Gan' Eden Takhton
The lower Garden of Eden
In the lower *Gan 'Eden*, the *Neshamot* (souls) are enjoying spiritual pleasures but still have a spiritual body resembling their former bodies.

גשמיות
Gashmiut
Corporeality
The possibilities of existence for separated entities became possible, only once distanced from the intensity of His light. The greater the distance more is the corporality possible.

דו"ן
D"uN
Masculine and feminine
Initials

דוכרין ונוקבין
Dukhrin Ve Nukvin
Masculine and feminine
See Mayin Dukhrin, Mayin Nukvin

דומם, צומח, חי, מדבר
Domem, Tsomeakh, 'Hay, Medaber
Mineral, vegetal, animal and the spoken
In parallel to the four worlds of *Atsilut*, *Beriah*, *Yetsirah* and *'Asiah,* there are four types of existence in our world: mineral (דומם), vegetal (צומח), animal (חי), and the speaking (מדבר).

דעת
Da'at
Sephira (Knowledge)
Fourth of the *Sephirot.*

דעת
Da'at
Knowledge
he essential knowledge is the one of the will of the Creator and His ways of guidance in this existence, as explained in the Kabbalah.

הארה
Hearah
Illumination
Special outburst of a light for a specific purpose.

הוד
Hod
Sephira – Glory
Eighth of the *Sephirot.*

הוי"ה
HaVaYaH

One of the ways of mentioning the Tetragamon
יְ-ה-ו-ה without pronouncing it.

היכל
Hekhal
Portal – Level
The *Hekhalot* are the different levels of ascension of the *Tefilot* before reaching the *'Olam Atsilut* during the *Amidah*.

הנהגה
Hanhagah
Guidance
The guidance of the worlds is done through the influence of the different *Sephirot* and *Partsufim* *(configurations)*.

הרחקה
Har'hakah
Distancing
Distance denotes a contrary or a non compatibility.
The possibilities of existence for separated entities became possible, only once distanced from the intensity of His light.

השגה
Hasagah
Attainment – Comprehension
To reach a higher level of understanding or comprehension, one has to make the effort of studying the *Sod* (secret) of the Torah which is the Kabbalah.

השתלשלות
Hishtalshelut
Evolution - Chain of events
In the Kabbalah the *Hishtalshelut* is the chain of events starting from the first act of G-od in this creation which is the "*Tsimtsum*" *(retraction)*, until the complex arrangements that make the guidance of the worlds.

ז' מלכים
Sheva' Malkhin
Seven kings
The seven kings of Edom that died (Bereshit, 36, 31), correspond to the seven lower *Sephirot* that broke during the *Shvirat HaKelim* (breaking of the vessels).

ז"א
Z"A
Zeir Anpin (Small countenance)
Initials of *Partsuf Zeir Anpin*, used more often than the full name.
See Zeir Anpin

ז"ת
Za"T
Zain Takhtonot
Seven lower *Sephirot*

זו"ן

Z"UN
Zeir Anpin and Nukvah
Initials of *Partsuf Zeir Anpin and Nukvah*, used more often than the full names.

זוהר
Zohar
The book of splendor, written by Rabbi Shim'on Bar Yo'hay.
The *Zohar* is the esoteric and mystical explanation of the Torah, and the base for most of the Kabbalah writings.

זיו
Ziv
Radiance – Illumination
A superior light will illuminate to a lower one to influence it, or to create a new emanation.

זיווג
Zivug
Union
The *Zivug* is the union of the masculine with its feminine. All the outcomes of the higher emanations are a result of the different unions of the masculine and feminine lights.

זין תחתונות
Zayin Takhtonot
Seven lower
The seven lower *Sephirot:*
'Hesed, Gevurah, Tiferet, Netsa'h, Hod, Yesod, Malkhut.

זכר
Zakhar
Masculine

There are masculine *Partsufim* that bestow kindness, and feminine *Partsufim* that bestow rigor. By their union, different equilibriums of these two forces (kindness and rigor), make the guidance.

זעיר אנפין
Zeir Anpin
Partsuf Zeir Anpin (Small countenance)

Zeir Anpin (Z"A) is composed of the seven lower *Sephirot: 'Hesed, Gevurah, Tiferet, Netsa'h, Hod, Yesod* and *Malkhut* of a world.

חבד
'HaBaD
'Hokhma, Binah and Da'at

Initials of the first triplet of the *Sephirot: 'Hokhma, Binah and Da'at.*

חגת
'HaGaT
'Hesed, Gevurah and Tiferet

Initials of the second triplet of the *Sephirot: 'Hesed, Gevurah and Tiferet.*

חומר
'Homer
Material – Physical

Materiality is only found in the lower world of *'Asiah* – action.

חוץ
'Huts
Outside
Denotes a position of non-compatibility or a contrary.

חושך
'Hoshekh
Darkness
State of distance from the *Kedushah* and closeness to the *Sitra A'hra* (negative side).

חיבור
'Hibur
Attachment
All the *Sephirot* and *Partsufim* have a certain degree of attachment between them.

חיה
'Hayah
Fourth level of the soul
'Hayah is the fourth level and can only be acquired after the preceding levels.

חיות
'Hayut
Livelihood
The livelihood of everything, whether positive or negative has only one origin; G-od the Creator and sustainer of all.

חיצוניות
'Hitsoniut
Exteriority (The)

The external or negative force – *Sitra A'hra* is also called exteriority.

חכמה
'Hokhma
Sephira – Wisdom
Second of the *Sephirot*.

חכמת האמת
'Hokhmat HaEmet
Knowledge of the truth
One of the names of the Kabbalah.

חלל
'Hallal
Space – Vacuum
The space left by the *Tsimtsum* (retraction) of His light.

חסד
'Hesed
Bounty – Kindness
Kindness is manifested by the different positioning and interaction of the masculine and feminine *Partsufim*.

חסד
'Hesed
Sephira (Bounty)
Fourth of the *Sephirot*.

חסד, גבורה, תפארת
'Hesed, Gevurah and Tiferet
Second triplet of the *Sephirof*.

טמא
Tameh
Impure
State of distance from the *Kedushah* and closeness to the *Sitra A'hra* (negative force).

י-ה ו ה
Adona-y
Y-H-V-H Tetragamon (י-ה-ו-ה)
Main name of G-od, reveals kindness and mercy, represented by the *Sephira Tiferet.*
The creative forces or energies are the different powers in the letters of the name of G-od י-ה-ו-ה, and the various letters added to make their different spellings.

יום
Yom
Day
Each new day, is of a new emanation that governs it.

יחוד
Yi'hud
Unification – Union
The union of the *Sephirot* or *Partsufim* for the *Zivug* and for the descent of the abundance.

יחודו
Yi'hudo
His unicity
The light of G-od is unique, of equal force, quality and

beyond all description.

יחידה
Ye'hidah
Fifth level of the soul
Ye'hidah is the fifth level and can only be acquired after the preceding levels.

יסוד
Yesod
Sephira (Foundation)
Ninth of the *Sephirot*.

יצירה
Yetsirah
World of formation – of the angels
The third world to unfold is called *Yetsirah*; the world of formation, the world of the angels. It is under *Atsilut* and *Beriah* and on top of *'Asiah*.

יצר
Yetser
Instinct – Impulse
The *Yetser Hatov* corresponds to the good or positive impulse in man, the *Yetser Hara'* is his bad or negative impulse.

ירושלים
Yerushalaim
Jerusalem
The closest place to G-od's emanations.

ישסו"ת

ISOT
Partsufim Israel Saba and Tevunah
Initials

ישסו"ת ב
ISOT 2
Second Partsufim of Israel Saba and Tevunah
Initials

כוונה
Kavanah
Intention – Concentration
Kavanah is to understand the words, and concentrate on the intention of the blessing or the *Tefilah* (prayer).

כחב
Ka'HaB
Keter, 'Hokhma, Binah
Initials

כיסא
Kisey
Throne
There are three main types of thrones:
Kisey HaDin - throne of justice
Kisey Hakavod - throne of glory
Kisey Ra'hamim - throne of mercy

כלי
Keli
Recipient –Vessel
Each *Sephira* is composed of a vessel called *Keli*, which holds its part of light called *Or*.

כתר
Keter
Sephira – Crown
First and most important of the *Sephirot*.

כתר, חכמה, בינה
Keter, 'Hokhma, Binah
The three first *Sephirot*, often referred as the *Ga'R*;
Shalosh Rishonot (the three first ones).

לאה
Leah
Leah - Partsuf Nukvah
The *Partsuf Nukvah* comprises of two distinct
Partsufim (configurations): *Ra'hel* and *Leah, Partsuf
Leah* of the aspect of rigor.

להחמיר
LeHa'hmir
To be more stringent
A strict observance of all the details when
accomplishing a *Mitsva* or *Tefilah*.

לוצאטו
Luzzatto
Rabbi Moshe 'Haim Luzzatto – Ram'hal
Born in Padua, Italy in 1707, died in Israel in 1746.
Rabbi Moshe 'Haim Luzzatto was a very prolific writer
and wrote on the all aspects of the Torah and the
Kabbalah.

לקבל
Lekabel
To receive
The word Kabbalah comes from the verb *Lekabel* (to

receive), but to receive it is first necessary to want, and to become a *Keli* (recipient) able to receive and contain this knowledge.

מ"ה
MaH (45)
Miluy (spelling) of the name י-ה-ו-ה *with a total of 45*
The name of *MaH (45)* is the *Miluyim* (spelling) of א, which is a (ו) (Vav) line in the middle (mercy) that unites two י (Yud) (kindness and rigor). It is of a masculine aspect and represents mercy.

מ"ן
M"N
Mayin Nukvin (feminine waters)
Initials

מוחין
Mo'hin
Brains
The *Mo'hin* are the directive force given to the *Partsuf* (configuration).

מיין דוכרין
Mayin Dukhrin
Masculine waters
One of two emanations allegorically called masculine waters.

מיין נוקבין
Mayin Nukvin
Feminine waters
One of two emanations allegorically called feminine waters.

162

מילוי
Miluy
Spelling
Depending on which letters are used, the numerical value of a name changes, and each one of these possibilities becomes different in its nature and actions.

מלאכים
Malakhim
Angels
The world of the angels is the third world; '*Olam Yetsirah* - the world of formation.

מלכות
Malkhut
Sephira (Royalty)
Tenth of the *Sephirot*.

מעשה בראשית
Ma'ase Bereshit
Works or acts of the creation
Name given for all the details of the beginning of the creation, from the *Tsimtsum*, the first worlds, the *Sephirot* etc.

מעשה המרקבה
Ma'ase Hamerkava
Works or acts of the Heavenly Chariot
Name given for all the details of the *Sephirot, Partsufim, Tikunim* and *Zivugim* that make the guidance.

מצוה

Mitsva

Commandment

As there are 613 *Mitsvot,* there are 613 veins and bones to man, 613 parts to the soul, and each *Sephira* and *Partsuf* also has 613 parts. This number is not arbitrary as there are important interrelations and interactions between them.

מקובל

Mekubal

Kabbalist - Accepted

A *Mekubal* is a person who is accepted to receive this knowledge, and is able to hold it by living in the path of Torah and rightness to strengthen constantly.

מקום

Makom

Place – space

Until the world was created, He and His Name were One. He willed to create, and contracted His light to create all beings by giving them a space.

מקור

Makor

Source – Origin

Each emanation has its source in the higher realms

מרקבה

Merkavah

Heavenly chariot

The *Partsufim* (configurations), *Sephirot* and the *Sephirot* tree, with all their inter-relations, actions and illuminations.

משל
Mashal
Allegory
Sometimes used to explain or illustrate difficult concepts.

מתלבש
Mitlabesh
Dress
Partsufim dress on, or in, each other. The more important *Partsuf* will dress inside the less important to direct him.

נהי
NeHY
Netsa'h, Hod and Yesod
Initials of the third triplet of the *Sephirot*: *Netsa'h, Hod and Yesod*.

נוטריקון
Notrikun
Acronym
Notrikun is a method of interpretation in which initials of different words make a new word.
אל מלך נאמן = אמן

נוקבא
Nukvah
Feminine - Sephira Malkhut – Partsuf Ra'hel, Leah
The *Partsuf* (configuration) *Nukvah* represents the feminine – the principle of receiving. It comprises of two distinct *Partsufim*: *Ra'hel* and *Leah*.

ניצוצות
Nitsutsot

Sparks

To sustain the *Kelim* after they broke, 288 sparks of their lights came down as well, because a connection to their original lights was needed to keep them alive.

נמשל
Nimshal
Moral
Sometimes used to explain or illustrate difficult concepts.

נפש
Nefesh
Soul - First level of the soul
Nefesh is the first level and lower level of the soul.

נפש, רוח, נשמה, חיה, יחידה
Nefesh, Rua'h, Neshama, 'Hayah and Ye'hidah
The soul has five names: *Nefesh*, *Rua'h*, *Neshama*, *'Hayah* and *Ye'hidah*, which correspond to its five levels. The soul is the spiritual entity inside the body, the latter being only his outer garment.

נצח
Netsa'h
Sephira (splendor)
Seventh of the *Sephirot*.

נקבה
Nekevah
Female – Feminine
Rigor is manifested by all the feminine aspects and by the concealment of the masculine aspects, which represent bounty.

נקודות
Nekudot

Punctuation – Vowels – Points

Each vowel corresponds to a *Sephira*. It in a way translates, with the combination of the letters, the inner identity of the word.

נר"ן
NaRaN

Nefesh, Rua'h, Neshama

Initials of the first three levels of the souls.

נשמה
Neshama

Soul - Third level of the soul

Neshama is the third level and can be acquired only after acquiring the level of *Nefesh* and *Rua'h*.

ס"ג
SaG (63)

Miluy (spelling) of the name י-ה-ו-ה with a total of 63

The name of *SaG* is the second level of the four names for a total of 63.

סגולה
Segulah

Remedy – Protection

Names, or combinations of names of angels with special signs or incantations, written on parchment to protect, or to invoke particular powers.

סודות
סוד -
Sod - ot

Secret –s

Through the knowledge of Kabbalah, we can get to a level of true understanding, and in a way "decode" the profound secrets of the Torah.

סיטרא אחרא
Sitra A'hra
Negative force
The root of the *Sitra A'hra* is in the lack, or absence of the *Kedushah*.

ספירה
Sephira
The light of G-od is unique and of equal force and quality. A *Sephira* is in a way a "filter" which transforms this light in a particular force or attribute, by which the Creator guides the worlds.

ספירות
Sephirot
Plural of Sephira
See Sephira

ספירות הישר
Sephirot HaYashar
Straight Sephirot
Sephirot arranged in three columns: right, left and middle, representing the guidance of the world in the manner of kindness, rigor and mercy.

ספירות העיגולים
Sephirot Ha'Igulim
Encircling Sephirot
These ten *Sephirot* are in charge of the general guidance of the worlds, and are not influenced by

the actions of men.

ע"ב
'A"V

Miluy (spelling) of the name י-ה-ו-ה with a total of 72

The name of *'A"V* is of the highest level of the four names of *'A"V, SaG, MaH (45)* and *BaN (52).*

עב, סג מה, בן
'A"V, SaG, MaH, BaN

Spellings of the Name י-ה-ו-ה

'A"V (72), SaG (63), MaH (45), BaN (52)

The creative forces or energies are the different powers in the four letters of the name of G-od י-ה-ו- ה, and the various letters added to make their different spellings.

עבודה
'Avodah

Service – Duty

One of the main goals of all the works, deeds and prayers of men in this existence, is to help and participate in the ascent of the fallen 288 sparks to their origin.

עולם
'Olam

World

A *'Olam* is a possibility and a type of existence, in a particular dimension.

עשיה
'Asiah

World of action – of man

The fourth world to unfold is called *'Asiah* - action, the world of physical existence.

עשר
'Eser
Ten
Number of *Sephirot* in each world, in each *Sephira, Partsuf*
or configuration.

עת
'Et
Time – Moment
Each moment can be described in term of permutation of
the names of G-od, and by the various *Sephirot and
Partsufim.*

עתיק יומין
'Atik Yomin
Partsuf – Ancient
The *Partsuf 'Atik* is superior to all the *Partsufim.*

פנימיות
Pnimiut
Internality
What is inside or interior. Also applies to deeper meaning or
spirituality.

פרצוף
Partsuf
Configuration - Countenance
A *Partsuf* is a configuration of one or more *Sephirot* acting
in coordination.

פרצופים
Partsufim
Configurations
See Partsuf

צדיק
Tsadik
Righteous
State of outmost closeness to the *Kedushah* and distance
from the *Sitra A'hra (negative force)*. Also attributed to the
Sephira Yesod.

צינור
Tsinor
Conduit
A *Sephira* is in a way a "conduit" which transforms the light
in a particular force or quality, by which the Creator guides
the worlds.

צל"ם
Tselem
Mo'hin (brains) of Z"A
The *Tselem* are the directive force - *Mo'hin* (brains) given to
Z"A.

צמצום
Tsimtsum
Contraction – Retraction
The "*Tsimtsum"* is the first act of the *Ein Sof* (Infinite) in the
creation. It is the retraction of His light from a certain space
and encircling it, so as to reduce its intensity and allow
created beings to exist.

קבלה
Kabbalah
The Kabbalah is the mystical and esoteric explanation of
the Torah. It teaches the unfolding of the worlds, the various
ways of guidance of these worlds, the role of man in the
creation, the will of the Creator and so on.

קבלה מעשית
Kabbalah Ma'asit
Practical Kabbalah
The "other" type of Kabbalah, where names or combinations of names of angels are used with special signs or incantations, sometimes written on parchment, to invoke particular powers and alterate normal states of events.

קדוש
Kadosh
Holly – Saintly
State of closeness to the *Kedushah* and distance from the *Sitra A'hra* (negative force).

קדוש ברוך הוא
Kadosh Barukh Hu
Saintly and Blessed He is
One of the names of G-od.

קדושה
Kedushah
Sanctity – Holiness
By accomplishing the *Mitsvot* and the *Tefilot* (prayers), men do the *Tikunim* (rectifications) necessary to detach the *Klipot* from the *Kedushah*. The ultimate goal is to create a maximum distance from the *Sitra A'hra* (negative force), and closeness to the *Kedushah*

קו
Kav
Ray – Line
Ray of light that emerged from the *Ein Sof* (infinite) and entered on one side of the *"'Hallal"* (vacant space)

172

קודשא בריך הוא
Kudsha Berikh Hu
Saintly and Blessed He is
See Kadosh Barukh Hu

קליפות
Klipot
Husks (negative forces)
The *Klipot* are the manifestation of the negative force.

קלקול
Kilkul
Deterioration – Damage
Kilkul is the opposite of *Tikun* (rectification).

קמיע
Kmi'a
Amulet
Names, or combinations of names of angels, with special signs or incantations, written on parchment to protect or to invoke particular powers.

רוח
Rua'h
Soul - Second level of the soul
Rua'h is the second level and is acquired before the next levels.

רוחני
Ru'hani
Spiritual
A spiritual person will give importance to this higher meaning of things, and live in the path of rightness to strengthen himself constantly.

רחל
Ra'hel
Ra'hel - Partsuf Nukvah
Partsuf Ra'hel is of the aspect of kindness .

רמח"ל
Ram'hal
Initials of Rabbi Moshe 'Haim Luzzatto

רע
Ra'
Evil – Bad
See Sitra A'hra

רפ"ח נצוצות
Rapa'h Nitsutsot
288 sparks
See Nitsutsot

רצון להשפיע
Ratson Lehashpia'
Will to bestow
The will of the Creator is to bestow goodness on His creatures.

רצון לקבל
Ratson Lekabel
Desire to receive
By his nature man is himself a *Keli* (recipient) with a will to receive without limits.

רשימו
Reshimu
Imprint – trace

Imprint of the first light that remained inside.

שבירת הכלים
Shvirat HaKelim
Breaking of the vessels
The seven lower *Sephirot* that could not hold the influx of their lights and broke.

שבת
Shabbat
The seventh day, *Shabbat* corresponds to the seventh *Sephira*; *Malkhut*.

שורש
Shoresh
Root
Every thing and existence has its root in the higher realms.

שכינה
Shekhina
Divine presence
One of the names of G-od.

שכר
Sakhar
Reward
The variable guidance is on the basis of justice, reward and punishment and is dependant on the actions of man. This guidance is by the linear *Sephirot*.

שער
Sha'ar
Gate – Portal
Entrance to a dimension. Gate to enter a knowledge.

תא חזא
Ta 'Haze
Come see (pay attention)
Expression frequently used in the *Zohar*.

תורה
Torah
The Kabbalah is the mystical and esoteric explanation of the *Torah*. All the profound secrets explained in the Kabbalah, are alluded in the letters, words and different stories narrated in the *Torah*.

תחית המתים
T'hiyat ha Metim
Resurrection of the dead
Final goal of the six thousand years.

תיקון
Tikun
Rectification or action
In Hebrew, the word "*Tikun*" has different meanings. It can be understood as reparation or rectification but also as function, relation or action.

תפארת
Tiferet
Sephira (beauty)
Sixth of the *Sephirot*.

תפילה
Tefilah
Prayer
The order of the *Tefilot* is based on the systems of ascension of the worlds, as explained in the Kabbalah.

תפילות
Tefilot
Prayers

תרי"ג
Taryag
613

There are 613 veins and bones to man, similarly, there are 613 *Mitsvot,* 613 parts to the soul, and 613 lights in each *Sephira*, this number is not arbitrary, as there are important interrelations and interactions between them.

Bibliography

From the Ram'hal

כללות האילן הקדוש
פתחי חכמה ודעת
קלח פתחי חכמה
כללים ראשונים
אדיר במרום

From the Ari Z'al

כתבי האריי
עץ חיים
שער רוח הקודש
שער הגלגולים

ספר הזהר
The Zohar
Rabbi Shim'on Bar Yo'hai

The Kabbalah of the Ari Z'al, according to the Ramhal
Rabbi Raphael Afilalo, Kabbalah Editions

Kabbalah Dictionary and Kabbalah Glossary
Rabbi Raphael Afilalo, Kabbalah Editions

דרך חכמת האמת לרמחל
Rav Mordekhai Chriqui, Editions Ramhal, Jerusalem

האילן הקדוש לרמחל
Rav Shalom Oulman (Jerusalem)

Index

''A, 169

'A"V, 32, 53, 169

'Hallal, 52

Abah, 70, 71, 80, 81, 83, 115, 143, 183, 186

Action, 31, 45, 60, 61, 69, 82, 102, 104, 109, 131, 146, 155, 169, 176

Adam Kadmon, 54, 68, 69, 143, 144

Angels, 20, 27, 28, 31, 37, 60, 127, 131, 132, 146, 147, 159, 163, 167, 172, 173

Ari Z'al, 21, 23, 24, 27, 31, 48

Arikh Anpin, 70, 80, 81, 83, 146, 186

Asiah, 102, 131, 145, 146, 147, 151, 159, 169

'Atik, 70, 80, 81, 170, 186

'Atik Yomin, 70, 80, 81, 170, 186

Atsilut, 102, 144, 145, 146, 147, 151, 152, 159

Autiot, 45

BaN, 28, 54, 75, 79, 92, 147, 148, 169

Beriah, 102, 131, 145, 146, 147, 151

Binah, 54, 69, 71, 72, 74, 81, 83, 143, 147, 148, 155, 160, 161, 188

Comprehension, 46, 47, 97

Created, 37, 51, 52, 84, 148

Creation, 19, 28, 37, 45, 51, 52, 55, 60, 61, 66, 69, 75, 82, 93, 102, 131, 146, 147, 153, 163, 171, 188

Creator, 28, 51, 93, 94, 111, 122, 127, 148, 174

Creatures, 28, 84, 86, 93, 174

Da'at, 71, 151

Ein Sof, 47, 69, 145, 171, 172

Emanation, 145

Evil, 37, 54, 60, 127, 128

Forces, 28, 31, 37, 43, 46, 91, 93, 97, 101, 143, 155, 173

G"aR, 148

Gevurah, 47, 69, 70, 71, 72, 73, 74, 75, 79, 81, 92, 103, 145, 148, 149, 154, 155, 157

Gevurot, 45

Gilgul, 121, 149

G-od, 144, 145, 158, 164

Growth, 69, 83

Guidance, 28, 37, 46, 56, 68, 80, 84, 86, 91, 93, 94, 97, 101, 104, 110, 122, 152, 155, 168, 175

Guided, 37, 93

HBD, 155

Hekhal, 103, 104

Hekhalot, 104

'Hesed, 70, 71, 72, 73, 74, 75, 79, 81, 91, 103, 154, 157

HGT, 155

Hokhma, 54, 70, 71, 72, 73, 74, 75, 81, 83, 143, 145, 148, 157, 160, 161

'Ibur, 121, 149

Imah, 80, 81, 83, 143, 145, 186

Influence, 93, 97, 101, 104, 110, 152

ISOT, 81, 159, 160

Israel Saba, 81, 159, 160

Kabbalah, 19, 32, 37, 43, 46, 47, 93, 97, 143, 145, 157, 161, 171

Kabbalist, 23, 24, 48, 146, 164

Kav, 69, 172

Kavanah, 160

Kedushah, 29, 127, 128, 156, 158, 171, 172

Keli, 19, 22, 65, 160, 161, 174

Kelim, 54, 55, 56, 165

Keter, 54, 65, 70, 71, 73, 74, 75, 81, 144, 148, 160, 161, 188
Klipot, 97, 127, 128, 172, 173
Knowledge, 19, 28, 161
Leah, 75, 81, 84, 161, 165, 174
Lekabel, 19, 161, 174
Levels, 28, 43, 60, 93, 97, 104, 115, 116, 128, 131, 145, 152, 166
Levush, 165
limit, 47, 145, 148
MaH, 28, 72, 73, 74, 79, 162, 169
Malkhut, 74, 81, 103, 144, 154, 163, 165, 175
Man, 28, 29, 31, 37, 44, 61, 79, 80, 91, 93, 94, 97, 101, 110, 111, 116, 122, 123, 127, 128, 144, 159, 163, 169, 175, 177
Mayim Nukvin, 162
meditation, 102, 148
Miluim, 46, 162
Miluy, 70, 71, 72, 73, 74, 75, 147, 162, 163, 167, 169
Miluyim, 53, 162
Mitsvot, 29, 44, 84, 85, 87, 97, 101, 104, 163, 172, 177
Mo'hin, 71, 85, 162, 171
Nekudot, 45, 167
Neshama, 29, 115, 116, 166, 167
Neshamot, 29, 30, 146, 149, 150
NHY, 85, 165
Nitsutsot, 55, 165, 174
Nukvah, 70, 71, 75, 80, 81, 84, 86, 101, 102, 153, 161, 163, 165, 174
Or, 144, 160
Partsuf, 82, 83, 84, 85, 143, 145, 146, 153, 155, 161, 162, 165, 170, 174
Partsufim, 23, 45, 46, 48, 59, 66, 75, 80, 81, 83, 84, 85, 86,

87, 91, 92, 98, 115, 116, 128, 143, 155, 157, 159, 160, 161, 163, 164, 165, 170
Pillars, 145
Punishment, 60, 91, 175
Ratson, 103, 174
Receive, 19, 28, 93, 94, 161, 174
Reshimu, 68, 174
Resurrection, 55, 112, 123
Reward, 60, 91, 175
rigor, 28, 47, 54, 66, 71, 72, 73, 74, 79, 80, 86, 87, 91, 92, 144, 145, 147, 148, 155, 161, 162, 174, 188
rigors, 45, 66, 71, 188
Rigors, 65, 92, 148, 149, 166, 185
Rua'h, 70, 71, 72, 73, 74, 76, 115, 116, 157, 166, 173
SaG, 71, 169
Sepher Hayetsira, 32
Sephira, 32, 33, 44, 46, 47, 79, 83, 92, 143, 144, 145, 147, 148, 149, 151, 157, 158, 159, 160, 161, 163, 165, 166, 167, 168, 170, 171, 175, 176, 177
Sephirot, 21, 23, 31, 32, 33, 45, 46, 48, 54, 55, 59, 65, 66, 68, 70, 71, 72, 73, 74, 75, 79, 81, 85, 91, 97, 116, 127, 128, 131, 144, 145, 147, 148, 149, 151, 153, 154, 157, 159, 161, 163, 164, 166, 168, 170, 175, 176, 188
Shvirat HaKelim, 54, 55, 109, 153
Sitra A'hra, 54, 127, 132, 156, 158, 168, 171, 172, 174
Souls, 37, 60, 115, 147
System, 37, 93, 97
Ta'amim, 45
Tagin, 45
Tefilah, 101, 102, 104, 105, 160, 161, 165, 176, 177

Tefilot, 31, 44, 80, 84, 85, 87, 97, 101, 103, 104, 152
Tevunah, 81, 159, 160, 186
Tiferet, 69, 70, 71, 74, 75, 81, 154, 155, 157
Tikun, 28, 29, 54, 55, 102, 116, 121, 148, 149, 173, 176
Tikunim, 32, 45, 85, 97, 109, 117, 121, 163, 172, 176
Torah, 29, 97, 176
Understand, 46, 55, 93, 97, 101, 104
Understanding, 69, 147
Will, 28, 31, 32, 52, 53, 55, 93, 94, 111, 112, 116, 122, 123, 127, 163, 174
World, 37, 55, 56, 59, 60, 61, 68, 80, 82, 84, 85, 86, 87, 91, 93, 102, 111, 116, 122, 127, 128, 131, 132, 146, 147, 151, 159, 163, 168, 169, 170

Worlds, 29, 37, 46, 52, 53, 54, 59, 60, 61, 65, 68, 69, 79, 82, 84, 85, 87, 91, 93, 97, 101, 102, 104, 110, 115, 127, 128, 132, 145, 146, 148, 151, 152, 168, 171
Ya'acov, 81
Yesod, 69, 70, 71, 73, 81, 103, 154, 159, 165, 171
Yetsirah, 102, 131, 145, 146, 147, 151, 159, 163
Yi'hud, 31, 158
Z'uN, 83
Z"A, 86, 153
Z"aT, 153
Zeir Anpin, 80, 81, 84, 85, 86, 102, 115, 153, 154, 155, 183
Zivug, 86, 105, 154
Zivugim, 30, 31, 45, 80, 84, 85, 86, 101, 102, 163

TABLES

Soul	World
Ye'hidah	Atsilut
'Hayah	Atsilut
Neshama	Beriah
Rua'h	Yetsirah
Nefesh	'Asiah

Soul	Configuration
Ye'hidah	Arikh Anpin
'Hayah	Abah
Neshama	Imah
Rua'h	Zeir Anpin
Nefesh	Nukvah

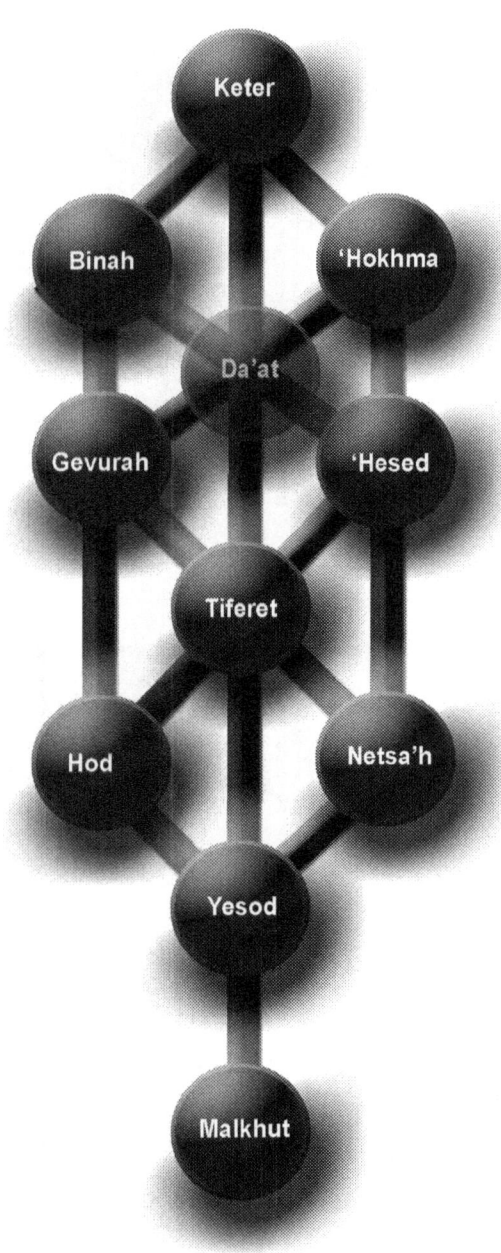

Sephira		Column	Position
Keter	Crown	Mercy	Center
'Hokhma	Wisdom	Kindness	Right
Binah	Understanding	Rigor	Left
Da'at	Knowledge	Mercy	Center
'Hesed	Bounty	Kindness	Right
Gevurah	Rigor	Rigor	Left
Tiferet	Beauty	Mercy	Center
Netsa'h	Glory	Kindness	Right
Hod	Splendor	Rigor	Left
Yesod	Foundation	Mercy	Center
Malkhut	Kingship	Mercy	Center

Sephira	Metal	Direction
'Hesed	Silver	South
Gevurah	Gold	North
Tiferet	Copper	East
Netsa'h	Tin	Above
Hod	Lead	Lower
Yesod	Silver	West
Malkhut	Iron	Center

Sephira	Level of the soul	Partsuf
Keter	Ye'hidah	'Atik Yomin Arikh Anpin
'Hokhma	Hayah	Abah Israel Saba
Binah	Neshama	Imah Tevunah
'Hesed	Rua'h	Zeir Anpin
Gevurah	Rua'h	Zeir Anpin
Tiferet	Rua'h	Zeir Anpin
Netsa'h	Rua'h	Zeir Anpin
Hod	Rua'h	Zeir Anpin
Yesod	Rua'h	Zeir Anpin
Malkhut	Nefesh	Nukvah

Sephira	Day
'Hesed	Sunday
Gevurah	Monday
Tiferet	Tuesday
Netsa'h	Wednesday
Hod	Thursday
Yesod	Friday
Malkhut	Shabbat

Sephira	Physical correspondence	Face
Keter	Head	Head
'Hokhma	Right brain	Right brain
Binah	Left brain	Left brain
'Hesed	Right arm	Right eye
Gevurah	Left arm	Right ear
Tiferet	Body	Right nostril
Netsa'h	Right leg	Left eye
Hod	Left leg	Left ear
Yesod	Masculine organ	Left nostril
Malkhut	Crown on the masculine organ	Mouth

Sephira	Tetragamon	
Keter	י	Extremity of Yud
'Hokhma	י	Yud
Binah	ה	First HeY
'Hesed	ו	Vav
Gevurah	ו	Vav
Tiferet	ו	Vav
Netsa'h	ו	Vav
Hod	ו	Vav
Yesod	ו	Vav
Malkhut	ה	Second HeY

Sephira	Quality
Keter	Complete kindness to all, even to the not deserving
'Hokhma	Kindness to all, even to the not deserving (but less than Keter, and not always)
Binah	Kindness to all, even to the less deserving (but from her, the rigors start)
Da'at	Guidance that makes the equilibrium between 'Hokhmah and Binah
'Hesed	Complete kindness to who is deserving
Gevurah	Full rigor to who is deserving
Tiferet	Kindness that makes the equilibrium between complete kindness and rigor
Netsa'h	Diminished kindness to who is deserving
Hod	Diminished rigor to who is deserving.
Yesod	Guidance that makes the equilibrium between Sephira Netsa'h and Hod
Malkhut	Guidance that translates all the superior emanations into one that is reflected to the creation Link or connection between all the superior Sephirot and man

לעלוי נשמת

Abraham David Hanania Afilalo bar Mira ז'ל

Salomon Afilalo ז'ל

Rav Abraham Chocron ז'ל

Mira Afilalo ז'ל

Gracia Chocron ז'ל

לעלוי נשמת

Sylvie Revah ז'ל

לעלוי נשמת

Rav Yeich Revah ז'ל
Joseph Revah ז'ל
Yacot Revah ז'ל
Israel Kakone ז'ל
Simi Kakone ז'ל
Mardoche Kakone ז'ל
Salomon Kakone ז'ל

With the compliments of

Armand & Ria Afilalo

With the compliments of

M. Gaby Bitton

לעלוי נשמת

שלמה בנדין ז"ל

With the compliments of

M. Gad Bitton

With the compliments of

M. Marc Kakon

With the compliments of

M. Jean Alloul

With the compliments of

Marc & Marie-Elaine Afilalo

With the compliments of

Judah & Katy Bendayan

With the compliments of

Sonia & Scott C. Swchartz

With the compliments of

Armand & Ria Afilalo